All my hope on God is founded; he doth still my trust renew,
me through change and chance he guideth, only good and only true.
God unknown, he alone calls my heart to be his own.

Mortal pride and earthly glory, sword and crown betray our trust;
though with care and toil we build them, tower and temple fall to dust.
But God's power, hour by hour, is my temple and my tower.

God's great goodness e'er endureth, deep his wisdom passing thought:
Splendor, light, and life attend him, beauty springeth out of nought.
Evermore from his store newborn worlds rise and adore.

Daily doth the almighty Giver bounteous gifts on us bestow;
his desire our soul delighteth, pleasure leads us where we go.
Love doth stand at his hand; joy doth wait on his command.

Still from earth to God eternal sacrifice of praise be done,
high above all praises praising for the gift of Christ, his son.
Christ doth call one and all: ye who follow shall not fall.

Robert Seymour Bridges (1844-1930)
ALT., AFTER JOACHIM NEANDER (1650-1680)

BALANCING ACT

How Women
Can *Lose*
Their Roles
& *Find* Their
Callings

MARY ELLEN ASHCROFT

InterVarsity Press
Downers Grove, Illinois

InterVarsity Press® is the book-publishing division of InterVarsity Christian Fellowship®, a student movement active on campus at hundreds of universities, colleges and schools of nursing in the United States of America, and a member movement of the International Fellowship of Evangelical Students. For information about local and regional activities, write Public Relations Dept., InterVarsity Christian Fellowship, 6400 Schroeder Rd., P.O. Box 7895, Madison, WI 53707-7895.

Scripture quotations, unless otherwise indicated, are taken from the New Revised Standard Version of the Bible, copyright 1989 by the Division of Christian Education of the National Council of the Churches of Christ in the USA. Used by permission. All rights reserved.

The author's research on Dorothy L. Sayers was supported by the Clyde S. Kilby Research Grant (1993) from the Marion Wade Center, Wheaton College.

Cover photograph: Ron Chapple/FPG International
ISBN 0-8308-1957-6

Printed in the United States of America ∞

Library of Congress Cataloging-in-Publication Data

Ashcroft, Mary Ellen, 1952-
   Balancing act: how women can lose their roles and find their
calling/Mary Ellen Ashcroft.
     p.   cm.
   Includes bibliographical references.
   ISBN 0-8308-1957-6 (paper: alk. paper)
   1. Women—Religious life.   2. Christian life.   I. Title.
  BV4527.A84   1996
  248.8'43—dc20   *96-1659*
                                           CIP

17	16	15	14	13	12	11	10	9	8	7	6	5	4	3	2	1
10	09	08	07	06	05	04	03	02	01	00	99	98	97	96		

*This book is dedicated to my wonderful husband Ernie,
who loves, supports and challenges me
in my balancing act.*

Preface

"I can't tell you how much I wish I'd read your book twenty years ago. I would have been spared a lot of pain." Jacky, an old high-school friend, lives in a small town in Washington State. She'd just finished reading *Temptations Women Face* when I visited her.

"You see, I'd completely lost myself. And I thought that was what a Christian woman was supposed to do. It was terrible. I got so low I felt like I was in a tunnel.

"And it was lonely. I felt I was the only one feeling like that, the only one who felt like I was going nuts. But what I really wanted to tell you was that I've started a nursery school in town—it's a dream I've always had—and along with nursery school there's a group for the mothers to talk about issues related to being mothers and women. I have the women in the group read your book. I don't want them to buy the lie that it's okay to lose themselves like I did. And I don't want them to feel so alone."

Christian women often feel alone in their struggle to balance their lives, to mother without losing themselves, to give themselves to home and family without losing sight of their God-given callings. Under intolerable pressure to be a certain kind of woman, they find themselves afraid to share deeply from their own life experiences. When you have to be good, nice, happy and contented (not to mention slim, well-dressed and in control), thinking and discussing big issues get tough.

My hope is that *Balancing Act* will encourage women to think about and discuss the big issues.

I have pulled from a number of sources for *Balancing Act*. My dependence on the Bible, my experience and the experience of other women will be obvious to readers. Much of the material on vocation comes out of my dissertation work on Dorothy L. Sayers. In her life and writing she explored issues of work and what it means for Christians to find their callings. (Thanks to the Marion Wade Center for awarding me the Clyde S. Kilby Research Grant for 1993 for my work on Sayers.) Much of the material in *Balancing Act* on the ways women's roles have been understood comes from other parts of my doctoral research.

And I have read widely in secular sources on issues related to women's development. I have tried to "eat the meat and spit out the bones." At the end of this book is a list of some of these books which women might find helpful for further reading.

Women need to consider the pressing demands they face, to ponder them deeply and discuss them with other women. To encourage your own reflection on some of these issues, I have included questions within many chapters. At the end of the book there is a set of discussion questions that are related to the questions in the chapters. I hope that reading *Balancing Act,* reflecting on your own balancing act and perhaps sharing with other women in group discussion will provide a rich, deepening experience as you follow Christ.

Note: When I refer to women in this book, I don't mean "women as opposed to men" unless I specify that. Some readers responded to parts of *Temptations Women Face* by saying, "You say here that women are often lacking in self-confidence. Well, I know men who are lacking in self-confidence too." That certainly may be, but I was focusing on women's lives in that book, and I am in this one. Women have always had to extrapolate from books on the "standard-model" male to their own lives. In *Balancing Act* I am writing about women's lives.

Part 1
Jesus Calls Women to Say Yes to Him & No to Others

1
The Call
of Jesus
to Follow

Now as they went on their way, he entered a certain village, where a woman named Martha welcomed him into her home. She had a sister named Mary, who sat at the Lord's feet and listened to what he was saying. But Martha was distracted by her many tasks; so she came to him and asked, "Lord, do you not care that my sister has left me to do all the work by myself? Tell her then to help me." But the Lord answered her, "Martha, Martha, you are worried and distracted by many things; there is need of only one thing. Mary has chosen the better part, which will not be taken away from her."
LUKE 10:38-42

*F*razzled and exhausted, Martha comes to Jesus. She wants an extra hand with supper; she wants to be able to keep her head above water, to cope so she can be a successful hostess for the evening.

Jesus refuses to give her what she wants. He looks straight past her momentary difficulty and sees a life fraught with distraction and anxiety. She wants someone to peel potatoes, and he offers her a focus for her days. She pleads for someone to set the table, and he hands her a firm foundation for her life.

Jesus tells Martha that there is need of only "one thing"; when she chooses the better part it will not be taken away from her. It will be something she can take with her throughout the varied changes of her years and into the life to come.

What is this "better part" that Mary has already chosen and Jesus offers Martha? What is the "good portion" that Jesus offers women today—within the frenzy of different voices demanding their time, distractions that seem to pull them this way and that, endless calls for their time from children's schools, jobs, homes, churches, neighbors? To what does Jesus call women, when we stop to hear his voice over the clamor of women's magazines, radio preachers, women's groups and talk-show hosts?

Following Jesus: that is the better part. Knowing and loving God and being known and loved by him: that is the better part. It is the life focused on him, sitting at his feet in love and dependence, seeking first the kingdom of God.

Well, that sounds simple enough.

But following Jesus has never been easy. It wasn't for Jesus' first followers, and it's not for women living today. It's easy enough to make an initial commitment to Jesus, but it's endlessly challenging to stay focused on him, to keep seeking his kingdom first, to continue making him our treasure and our prized possession. It's frustratingly easy, even for someone who has followed Jesus for years, to slip off-balance and lose that essential center in God.

Who knows if it's harder for us than it was for the early followers, distracted as we are by homes, children, parents, jobs and church activities? Sometimes I think it must have been easier for the thousands of women who entered cloistered nunneries, simpler for them to live the Christian life, to keep focused on Christ, because they didn't have myriad other urgent "good things" pulling them away from this most important "one thing." If I didn't want to get to know my neighbors; if I didn't want to feed my family healthy food; if I didn't care about cultivating a rich, growing relationship with my husband into our old age; if I didn't want to have some close friends to whom I am accountable; if I didn't feel a sense of call to serve in the church; if I didn't feel called to teach; if I didn't feel called to write—oh yes, then my life would be simple and I would sit for hours, days, months and years at the Lord's feet.

Day-to-Day, Year-to-Year Balancing

Dream on. For me, and for other women I know, the struggle is a day-to-day balancing act. It is the struggle to keep focused on Jesus even as we feel ourselves pulled apart by a hundred demands. It is the struggle to keep listening to Jesus, despite the many voices clamoring for our allegiance and obedience. Our walk with Jesus is a balancing act that never seems to quit. I can never say, "Now the kids are all out of diapers—now it will be easy to pray and put Jesus first." I can't say, "Now that I've quit my job (or started a job) it will be easier to stay on track and put first things first." Day in, day out, year in, year out, I need to keep finding ways of putting Jesus first, of finding his calling to me, of balancing my life.

Mary said yes to Jesus and no to things that would distract her from her first love. How do we find out how to follow Jesus, to listen for his voice, within our various life circumstances?

There's Kristi, who has always wanted to be a doctor. Her teachers have encouraged her to pursue medicine. She feels that she could really help people as a doctor. But she says to me, "I've got to be realistic. If I'm premed, guys will treat me like I'm too brainy. They'll feel inferior and run a mile. And how could I really be a doctor? Who'd look after the kids?" What does it mean for Kristi to follow Jesus?

There's Fiona. She'd always been told by her academic family that a person is nothing without a Ph.D. She'd studied for years, getting an M.A. in microbiology. In the middle of a Ph.D. program she became a Christian. Her studies seemed increasingly boring to her. Soon she found she didn't care about different genetic theories at all. She got married but keeps feeling under pressure to finish a dissertation, although she cares less and less about it. What she really wants is to have children and home-school them. How does Fiona decide how to follow Jesus?

There's Ursula. Her children are all at school, and she feels pressure to do something new. She considers resuming her education or doing volunteer work in a shelter for the homeless. But maybe she should stick with what she knows she can do well and have another baby. How does Ursula discern what voices she should listen to?

There's Heloise. She's always dreamed of finishing her college degree, and now her children are going away to college. Sometimes it almost seems like something she could do. But her friends whose children are at the same stage want her to get more involved in the tennis league and the bridge club. How does Heloise decide what to do?

There's Betty. She hates her job writing brochures for a large advertising company—brochures that are of questionable accuracy—and feels that she is being forced to compromise on the dreams she had of teaching high-school kids. Her parents keep telling her to stay in the job, at least until she can buy a car and maybe meet the right man. How does Betty follow Jesus in these circumstances?

There's Laura. She has finally reached her goal of being made a partner in her law firm. But when she has her first baby, she feels a sense of tremendous grief at the idea of leaving little Sara with a baby-sitter. Maybe she should put her career on hold. How does Laura know what following Jesus means?

There's Kim. She's always enjoyed being a homemaker, but the family needs another paycheck. She worries that she might not be able to get to all her daughter's basketball games or visit her ailing mother in the nursing home. How does Kim follow Jesus?

Standardizing the Call of Jesus

The call to discipleship is endlessly challenging, and we would prefer it to be easy. We'd like to standardize the call of Jesus. We love the voices that give us simple answers: "Women can do anything men can do. Go for it!" "Women need to find their whole fulfillment in their husbands, children and homes." Most of us have tried donning these one-size-fits-all garments once or twice in our lives. (In fact, women may more easily fall prey to these "easy answers" because we have been raised with less sense of who we are and what we will do. Most of us, unlike boys we grew up with, had no long-term dream, like "Someday I will become a cardiologist and study heart disease.") Couple this with the fact that most women carry a profound sense of self-doubt, and you have a recipe for disaster. In my experience, even the most competent and gifted woman feels that really she is pretending to be competent, that if anyone saw underneath the surface, they'd see how needy, how inadequate she is. So women, lacking long-term dreams and self-confidence, are vulnerable to the voices of experts telling them who they are and what they should do with their lives. *What do I know?* a woman says to herself.

What do we do when we begin to feel uncomfortable with some of these simple answers, when we sense that they don't fit and aren't true to life? What do I do when I see Jesus calling a woman to do something different from what he's called me to do?

Well, generally what Christian women have done is to judge and condemn each other. I can imagine Mary looking at Martha and thinking, *Honestly, what a ditz! All she ever thinks about is how long to cook potatoes and how much garlic to put in and what flowers will look nice on the table. Why doesn't she consider getting a life?* Meanwhile Martha was probably thinking, *How come I get a sister like this who's good for no earthly use? All she does is stare off with this dreamy expression. What a space cadet!* Of course Martha doesn't think of herself as "just a ditzy housewife." Nor does Mary consider herself a space cadet. But we love to pigeonhole and simplify each other, because then we can more easily dismiss and despise each other and ignore each other's challenge to us. After all, "she's just a _____."

Women judge each other, and they push for uniformity of life. Martha appeals to Jesus, asking him to get Mary to do exactly what she's doing (because if she's doing it, it must be right). Likewise, if a woman's doing something different from me—working outside the home and I'm not (or not working outside the home and I am)—I feel she must be wrong. Women who may be called to singleness find themselves being pushed to "standardize" by marriage. It seems to be very hard for us as Christian women to give each other freedom. We are quick to think that if a woman is doing something different from us, we should disapprove of her, and God almost certainly does too. If a woman changes from one vocation to another, following God's call, she should expect the support of her Christian sisters, not their suspicion and condemnation.

This book comes out of my strong conviction that Jesus calls us to follow him in ways that will look different at different times in our lives. It comes out of my own experience as full-time homemaker, full-time mother, minister's wife, teacher, student, mentor, daughter. And it comes from years of listening to students, members of many denominations, neighbors, colleagues and others.

I believe that the only way we can standardize the call of Jesus is to say that it is a call to discipleship, a call to keep following, a call to keep growing and changing as we move along our lives with him. Jesus doesn't look for ways to simplify people and pigeonhole women.

To Jesus, Martha is not a "ditzy housewife." She is someone who has allowed herself to be pulled off-balance by her worries and distractions, a woman who needs to be brought back to focus. Instead of despising and dismissing her, Jesus looks for the best in her and calls that forth. He doesn't tell her to get a life; he gives her one. That's love.

The Call to Freedom

Ultimately, Jesus' call to follow is the call to freedom.

Saying yes to freedom means saying no to bondage. Saying yes to following Jesus means saying no to many of the other voices that seek to pull us off-balance: it is saying no to what Christians have often termed "the world."

In our society, for instance, the bank president who "pulls down three figures" is an important woman. But the real question, the crucial question she needs to face, pushes her deeper than the money she makes and the societal accolades she gets: Is she following Jesus? In the evangelical subculture, on the other hand, often the "real" woman is the one who gives herself fully to her home, husband and children. And the question she needs to face is identical to the one that the bank president faces: Is she following Jesus?

This book is about finding that freedom to follow. It is about turning a critical ear to the voices that have been clamoring at women, telling them how they should run their lives; it is about asking where those voices come from and how they square with the voice of Jesus. It is about listening for the call of Jesus to freedom.

For the voice of Jesus might inspire the bank president to quit her job and stay home with her babies. Or she might go to Africa and work in a hospital. The voice of Jesus might call the homemaker to give herself to working at a shelter or might inspire her to get a job at a university library. Or each of them might find God calling them to stay where they are, living and working for him, balancing their lives as they stay focused on him.

Probably both the homemaker and the banker would prefer to stay where they are. But Jesus calls us to keep growing. Most of us have days when we figure we'd like to stop following, when we wish that our present calling would stay that way forever and we didn't have to keep listening to the call of Jesus; we wish we could quit our growing-up process. We wish we could stop struggling to balance our lives as we follow Jesus, and simply stretch out in a recliner with the television on. Perhaps it's just as well that we are seldom given the option of getting too comfortable. Something comes along—an unruly boss, a difficult child, a financial problem, a sense of frustration—which tips us up out of our recliner and onto the floor. Then we realize that it's time to get moving again. Time to get on with our own individual balancing act, as we put first things first and follow Jesus.

Not What, but Why

In this book I want to push women not to get stuck on issues like "Should I work outside the home or not?" or "What kind of career is the one for me?" These are important areas, and in part three we will get practical as we look at balancing relationships, calling and work. But often people forget to move deeper than these pragmatic career-counseling questions. College students often feel they need to decide for a lifetime: "I need help figuring out what I should be doing with my life." Women who hear me speak on issues of calling ask me afterward, "I've been home for twelve years with kids and I need to decide what's next. Can you help me?" Or, "My job has taken over my life, and I need to decide whether to stay there or quit."

This basic question—"What should I be doing?"—seems very important to us; we are desperate to know. But my conviction is that choosing "the better part" has less to do with *what* we do than with *why* we do it. Jesus calls women away from the many things that would seek to scatter them; he calls them from distraction to focus. The trick is to figure out which is which. What may be a distraction at one time in a woman's life may be what she is called to focus on at another time.

"I've decided, just in the last month or two, to quit my youth program." Elaine looked toward me as we walked along. My face must have registered surprise. She had been a church accountant in a large California church, but her gifts with youth had surfaced as more and more kids pulled her away from her numbers to pour out their hearts. Finally the church staff had decided to recognize the inevitable, and they set her free to pursue a God-given calling. Over the years her work had turned into an after-school program in which she had helped hundreds of kids.

"You'll want to know why," Elaine continued. "For years now, every night when Bob comes home from work—he's been very supportive of my work, you know—but he gets home and we eat supper and he wants time with me. He's keen on biking, you know, and likes gourmet cooking and wants me to help him. And he likes to watch classic movies. As soon as we sit down I always fall asleep. I can't help but feel that since he really wants his wife's companionship . . . that it's really something I should do . . ." She paused and looked at me again.

"We had a church weekend, and the speaker talked about how women need to make sure they're under proper headship. And Bob really would like it . . . One of these days we might have grandchildren, and I'd like to be able to look after them . . ."

When Elaine told me that she was quitting her youth ministry so that she could join her husband in his hobbies, I admit that I was lost for words.

I knew many kids who had been helped by her listening, her program, her gentle advice and prayer. How could someone who seemed so wise be so confused?

I'm sorry to say that I was stunned into silence by Elaine's revelation. The only thing I could think to say (and I didn't have the nerve) was "Let me get this straight. You're telling me that Jesus came to earth in human flesh, died on the cross, so that you could keep awake to watch classic movies with your husband?"

That was six years ago, and I haven't talked to Elaine recently. I did get an apologetic message saying she'd been in town but hadn't had time to organize a visit—it seemed like since she had less to do she got a lot less done, she said.

Donna looked at me over the teapot. "I was about eight months pregnant with Lilly, and Fred was two. I was in the communications department, had just been made associate professor and was loving it. After the years of both Clint and I doing our doctoral work, life seemed great, and we liked the daycare person we'd found. She was great, and Fred seemed happy." Donna poured some tea.

"Then came the big day, or big night, really. This was thirteen years ago now, but I remember it very clearly. I was at a party at the home of one of the tenured professors. It was quite a crush—everybody was there. I spoke with a woman who'd been department chair for years and now was traveling all over the world related to a book she'd written—she must have been about fifty-five at the time. 'How long are you taking off?' she said, eyeing my bump. 'Eight weeks,' I said. 'Same as I took when Fred was born.' 'That's great,' she said to me. 'Glad to see you hanging in there. Exactly what I did.' She started to move away from me across the room and then turned. 'You know . . . I don't remember much about their childhoods though.' "

Donna brushed her graying hair back and smiled ruefully. "I went into work the next day and took a leave of absence. I didn't want to not remember my children's childhoods."

Donna quit her job almost thirteen years ago. She's been on several charitable boards since then and very active in her children's schools. Her time outside the work force has allowed her to develop a profound interest in issues related to children, especially poverty and literacy issues. She's looking for a job now, which will use some of the gifts she's always had, in light of this new area of interest.

Two women quit their jobs: exactly the same thing. They felt they wanted more time with family. But under the surface I believe that Elaine and Donna were doing exactly the opposite, because *why* they did it was completely different.

Moving beyond *what* we do to *why* we do it is crucial. Martha might have been commended for her hospitality, had she not been using it to feed her soul. Mary might, I guess, have been sitting at the Lord's feet for all the wrong reasons. Similarly, women today might be dedicated Christian homemakers for the right or wrong reasons; they might be high-powered executives for the right or wrong reasons. Each one needs to find the freedom to follow Jesus. She needs to ask, along with Martha and Mary, "How can I follow Jesus right now in my life?"

Elaine and Donna, Mary and Martha—all of them needed to be looking carefully beyond the *what* to the *why:* In doing what I'm doing, what am I trying to prove to whom?

For a woman to find freedom, to find balance, she must be rooted in the love of God. Without this foundation, she will use other things to feed her soul. She'll use her work or her relationships to make herself feel good. And in doing that, she will become fundamentally out of kilter, unbalanced.

As we will see, women have been told by the world and by the church that they are to be Marthas, scurrying around doing their duty, looking after people. While that may be many women's calling, if it doesn't come out of being a Mary—sitting at Jesus' feet and knowing oneself to be loved—it offers imbalance and bondage instead of balance and freedom.

Sometimes when I think about balancing my life, I imagine myself as a juggler with different balls in the air—family, work, exercise, spiritual life, hobbies. But I've realized that this is false. In fact my spiritual life, my discipleship, is the ground I stand on while juggling the balls. Or to shift the metaphor, my relationship with Christ is the water on which I paddle my canoe and keep my balance.

The issue here goes much deeper than women's careers or relationships. It is about a woman having a strong enough sense of herself as a disciple that she could quit a job (or pursue a new one) in response to the call of Christ. It is about a woman having enough sense of herself as a child of God that she doesn't engage in a desperate struggle to stay popular with her children or a frantic compromise to make herself attractive to a potential husband.

It is about having such solid roots that we will not be rocked. When our children leave for college, we will be touched, but not shaken from our foundation. If a spouse dies or leaves, or if we lose a job we really love, we will still know our ultimate security. If our life circumstances change and we decide to quit a job—to look after small children, aging parents, a sick spouse, or just to rethink priorities—the essence of who we are will not be taken away from us. Even if we experience great success, becoming a CEO or winning a Pulitzer Prize, we will find our security in God. Even when we learn of the terminal disease or slip into confusion in the nursing home, the essence of who we are as a child of God will be there as rocklike as ever.

This issue, then, is at the heart of women's lives. It is about the balance that comes when a woman knows she is loved by God and allows her calling to flow out of that love, instead of trying frantically (through her bank presidency or her housewifery) to make herself worthy of God's (and others') love. It is an issue of freedom, the freedom of discipleship, the freedom that comes when we lay aside our burdens and pick up the yoke of Jesus. It is about choosing the better part, which can never be taken away from us.

But as we shall see, saying yes to following Jesus is challenging, especially within the complexity of women's lives. And saying yes to the voice of Jesus demands that we discern the other voices, the voices of the world, which often sound very sweet and appealing to our ears. This will be our task in part one. In part two we will look more closely at what Jesus calls us to. And in part three we will look at practical ways to work out the balancing act, which is a life following Jesus.

2
Piecing
Together
a Godly Life

*O*h for the good old days, when families were families, and everybody knew just what role they were supposed to play . . . Or were they so good? Listen to these recollections of women about their childhoods.

☐ What I remember best about my early childhood is that my dad was never there. He worked long hours and then was out of town traveling a lot. When he was home, he seemed distant, sitting behind his paper or watching TV. My mom was there, but she was distracted—it seemed like we were always hanging out washing or grocery shopping . . . We never talked much.

☐ I could tell when my dad had been transferred again when I'd come in from school and my mom was cooking in silence, her mouth drawn like a straight line. Then when I was in bed, I'd hear their raised voices. After a while she stopped making friends in new

places and so did he. I heard later that companies moved their staff
around a lot so that the men would be more dedicated workers, not
distracted by social lives.

☐ Our neighborhood was empty of men all day. At about 4:30 or
5:00 p.m., a shiver of excitement went through the streets—the dads
were coming! We'd flurry around the house, tidying up and putting
toys away, parking bikes and scooters, while Mom had her apron
on, making supper. In the evenings or on the weekends, you sometimes saw men working in their yards. Occasionally you'd see one
playing catch with his son, but it was the moms who were with the
little ones at the playground. It was a very divided world. He had
his job, and she had hers.

Everyone knew what to do in the neatly structured, divided world
these women remember. The life of the successful man fit a standard
pattern, from point A to point B, like going on a trip from one city
to the next. Oh sure, he may have had to cross a bridge, perhaps
a mountain pass, and even fight with a bandit, but basically he
tooled along from one place to the next without false starts, de-
tours or changed routes. The man did well in high school, usually went
to college, began a professional life, married, had several children,
got promoted, moved around a bit, bought a house and a cabin or a
boat. Finally he retired, pruned roses and surveyed his accomplishments.

There were nice things about the security and the rigidity of this
kind of world. But the costs were too great. He never knew his children
and often took little time for his emotional or spiritual life. She spiraled into boredom and frustration. The children grew up primed for
rebellion.

Most women would not want to return to these days. And most men
wouldn't either. Many men have realized that work cannot be everything. You see more and more of them at the playgrounds with children, holding their babies, changing diapers, taking paternity leave.
And many Christian men are deciding that they need to take relationships and commitments more seriously.

Women don't want a divided life—either of the female or the male kind. They recognize that career is not enough; they want to be interconnected with people. They want to keep growing throughout their lives, adjusting as needed to different circumstances. They want to live a balanced life.

The Shawl or the Quilt

Women's lives are more like a wander in a garden than a journey from one city to another. A woman may go to school, start college, quit college and get married, have a child or two, go back to college to finish a degree, work at a job, have another child and stay at home and do interesting volunteer work, which inspires her to rethink her life, so she goes back to school in a different field . . .

Perhaps women's lives are like a woven shawl. Before I started to weave, I didn't realize how long it took to set up the warp for a weaving project. The weaver chooses strong yarn for the warp, and measures it carefully and sets it up on the loom, a process that can take a whole day. Only then can she start to weave.

These strong lines that run from the front to the back of the loom seem to me to be like a woman's earliest sense of her calling, her gifts, her sense of herself. On that warp, she begins to weave her life. The process is long. She chooses her weaving materials. She may pick a sturdy wool and then shift to a fluffy, warm mohair. She may decide she wants an undyed wool for a stretch in her life, and then shift to powerful reds and purples. She may, like Penelope in Homer's *Odyssey,* unweave some of what she weaves. If she stops and looks at her life, she will see a work of art in process on her loom.

Or a woman's life is like a quilt. Just as the quilt is made up of many scraps and materials, the batting for warmth and the backing to hold it all together, women's lives are made up of many components. A quilt doesn't work unless it is pieced together and unless it is stitched— thousands of stitches. A woman's life is made of many fabrics, and she stitches it over years.

The really beautiful quilts, the ones that win prizes in fairs and the ones that are exhibited in museums and passed on to children—these quilts are not all pastel shades of green and pink, or perfectly matched reds, whites and blues. They are drawn from the many colors of life's materials: from Jim's old flannel shirt, the Liberty fabric of Jenny's blouse, a bit of satin from the bridesmaid's dress of Flo's wedding. Sometimes, on a real work-of-art quilt, the colors seem to clash. What makes it shine as a work of art is the fact that it has been pieced together—all these diverse materials—with love and care and time. Women's lives can't be ordered from a magazine like a pastel quilting kit; they are pieced together from bright and dull, fine and coarse, fancy velvet and hard-wearing denim.

My husband and I lived in South Africa from 1974 to 1982. While I was pregnant with our second son, I decided to make a quilt. I had bags of scraps—all colors—from sewing projects I'd done, and even some from my mother's old sewing bags. For the star sections of the quilt I pieced together several diamonds, each of a different fabric— from the first dress I'd sewn in junior high to my great-aunt's favorite apron. Then I carefully sewed each star onto the center of an off-white square. I quilted each square separately with small designs in the corners and through the center star. Then it was time to piece the squares together.

We had very little money at the time, and I bought two sheets on the sale table at Stuttafords. The sheets were a kind of olive green, 60 percent cotton, 40 percent polyester. I cut one sheet into strips and saved the other one for the backing. I sewed the quilt top together and quilted it onto the back panel.

I looked at my project. There were many months of work here, years in fact. And I realized I'd made a big mistake. I'd taken a wrong turn with my green strips. I stared at it for hours and days, as I nursed my baby. The last thing I wanted to do was to start again.

But this quilt was like a woman's life. To get it right, I was going to have to go back, rip up the wrong stitches, change the colors that didn't work—because I wanted to get it right. I wanted it to be a work of art.

Piecing Together a Life

Karina is a friend of mine who knows the pain and the ultimate satisfaction of reworking her life quilt. Involved for years in a marriage to an abusive drug addict, Karina finally woke up to the danger she was in. Not only was she being physically abused, but she was at a point where she no longer had any self-respect. If someone asked her what she thought about something, she could hardly answer.

Karina moved out and got divorced. To support herself and her son, she got a job working in a jewelry store and started back to college to finish her degree in business. Just before she graduated, she met a widowed Christian man in the jewelry store, and they dated and got married. Karina found herself loving certain elements in her work, especially being there to talk to people at key points in their lives, when they were buying someone a special piece of jewelry. As she and her husband talked, she realized that the way she liked talking and listening to people and the way they poured out their hearts to her were indications of a God-given calling that she should consider. She is planning to get a master's in counseling and become a counselor.

Karina's situation ten years ago seemed hopeless. I couldn't have imagined her as she is today. And who knows where she will be tomorrow?

Like a woman quilting one hundred years ago from old scraps of torn clothing, women like Karina know how to improvise. They take the less-than-perfect materials they are handed, and make something beautiful.

Karina's life has changed radically. Her external circumstances are not what she started with. She has a different job, a different home and a different family life. She had to rip out some of her quilting. She had to unweave some of the weaving of her life.

Quilting Materials: Work, Calling and Identity

When I first met Karina, I asked her what she did. "I work in a jewelry store," she said.

She wasn't lying. But to define herself this way was far from the truth.

Work is often an important component of our lives, a key element in the quilt, but most women recognize that they cannot be defined by their work: it is not the whole story of their lives. Women don't want their success to be equated with the money they make. They don't want their answer to the question "What do you do?" to reflect solely the hours between eight and five. To look at women's balancing acts, to look at how women follow Jesus, we need to look at work. But work is the tip of the iceberg.

People's working lives are more complicated than they were in the days when Dad went off for long hours and Mom stayed home doing housework. Certainly, women's choices are greater. A generation ago a woman didn't have to decide whether she wanted to, say, go to a military academy or not. And more and more women work outside the home, from necessity or choice. Many women have realized that their unexamined expectation—that they will be supported by a man—is an illusion.

Work is a fact of life. It is, however, part of a greater project, that of weaving and piecing together a life. Work is an activity—paid or unpaid—which fills many of our hours. It is part of what is woven, but a woman's sense of calling is the warp onto which she weaves her days.

Work is not necessarily the same as our calling. Calling has more to do with the deep sense of our giftedness and our burning sense of what we must do with our lives. According to Frederick Buechner, "The place God calls you to is the place where your deep gladness and the world's deep hunger meet."[1] That is calling.

Some people have the delightful situation of their work being their calling. More—usually for financial or other circumstantial reasons—pursue their calling after they've earned their checks.

Vocation is a word drawn from the word *calling*. There are many who believe that some of the world's problems lie in our society's lack of a sense of vocation. In his famous book *Habits of the Heart,* Robert Bellah argues that when people have a sense of calling, work becomes morally intertwined with life and the self is seen as part of a disciplined community.[2] It is calling, says Alasdair MacIntyre, that is the link between the individual person and the larger community.[3] Without calling, work is simply what earns a buck.

A person's calling is intimately bound up with her identity—who she is, what she is gifted to do. Calling is the strong warp that runs throughout the weaving project; it is the background material for the quilt. We've all met people who spent their childhoods caring for doll injuries or baby birds and are now doctors, physical therapists or nurses. Or people who constructed elaborate building-block creations and then became architects or builders. In fact many career advisers suggest that women's callings will be best found when they recall childhood dreams and joys. (I'll talk about this more in part two.)

Calling is inextricably bound to identity. "In a calling," writes Bellah, "one gives oneself to learning and practicing activities that in turn define the self and enter into the shape of its character."[4] In pursuit of our God-given callings we come to know ourselves better.

A woman's identity, her authentic personhood, includes her gifts, the things she loves to do, the things that energize her. These, in turn, are part of her calling and may become her work. But for a person to be able to follow Jesus, she needs to have a sense of who she is (identity), and she needs to be pursuing her calling.

We're not talking here about "me" religion. The self, according to Robert C. Roberts, professor of philosophy and psychological studies at Wheaton College, is an idea that Christians need not fear:

> According to the Christian Word, the core of the selfhood of all of us—what we most truly are as selves, whether or not we have actualized and acknowledged this—is that we are bearers of God's image, made and intended to be his children, to love him and our neighbor and to serve in his kingdom. This is the self that Christian nurture promotes. . . . This self is sacrosanct in Christianity; it would always be wrong to deny one's nature as a child of God.[5]

Without a healthy sense of self, one's calling flounders. And without a firm sense of self, grounded in God, women's relationships easily sicken. We've all known a mother who gives and gives and gives. It all seems too good to be true, and sure enough, she is unable to let go of her children. Her husband raises certain topics for conversation, and she bursts into tears. Identity, authentic personhood, is crucial, because without it a woman is rootless, unable to stand firm through life's changing circumstances.

And a strong sense of identity is necessary for a woman to keep balance in her calling and work. Even with a powerful sense of her gifts and calling, the woman with little sense of identity is rudderless and unfocused.

I think of Tiffany, a brilliant actor, who also organizes school theaters. She has known her calling for over thirty years. She started acting when she was a child, and today she graces people's lives with her acting and her way of bringing drama to them. Yet when the slightest criticism comes her way, Tiffany falls apart or gets depressed. And her life has been a progression of unhappy relationships with men. Somehow she seems to attract men who treat her badly, two-time her and ultimately drop her. Calling and work are not what's missing. She may spend her life pursuing the next great compliment or rave review of her acting, thinking that those will make her happy, but they won't. She may pursue a man, hope to have a family, but these will not give her what she needs. A sense of identity, of joy in her own soul—that's what Tiffany lacks.

A person's life calling springs from the essential center of who she is. Karina loves to listen to people and help them see new possibilities for their lives. This is what women know as the central issue: it is about finding and knowing the self, about integrity, about staying true to this authentic personhood in a variety of life situations.

Karina's life is different now from the way it was ten years ago, and yet her calling and identity have not changed. What may have been a sleeping call—a love of people and an ability to listen to them, a way of seeing deeper into people's lives—surfaced until it was a compelling force in her life. Karina's calling shows in her way of relating to people even now, before she officially becomes a counselor and her calling overlaps with her work.

But as is the case for many women, Karina's sense of call needed help to be awakened. Her sense of herself had been so damaged that she needed to remember that she had value as a person, a child of God. Although she was "saved" before, she now knows herself as a person whom Jesus would call. She now knows her life as a work of art that she is creating in collaboration with God—the greatest creator-artist.

Pulled in Pieces

Many women lose all sense of who they are and what they are called to do.

When I began to consider, in 1984, the possibility of going back to school to finish my degree, the thought made me feel almost sick with terror.

I'll have you know that I was the perfect wife, mother, homemaker and minister's wife. Now with the kids getting a little older, I actually thought about what else I might do, maybe a part-time job as a secretary, or as a travel agent. After all, I'd traveled a lot. And I could type a bit.

But the sense of myself as someone who could do something—who had something she wanted to do—had been buried for over ten years. Not dull years. Eight of them were in South Africa, working with my Anglican minister husband in the church there, and raising our three children. But somehow my sense of myself had gotten lost.

In spite of my terror I started, over the next year, looking into various degree programs around the area. Of course I had to request transcripts from my early college days in Washington State (where I'd done almost three years of college without ever being quite sure why) and transcripts from the year's study I'd done at an Anglican seminary. I remembered then—vaguely—that I'd actually done quite well in school, that I'd enjoyed it. And yet it seemed like a miracle when a college accepted me.

I was going to major in elementary education. I had just barely enough nerve to go back to college, so I wanted to do something I could be sure I'd be competent at. I liked my own children, I was good at reading aloud, and I saw magazine articles noting the need for many elementary teachers in the next few years, so that settled it. It was safe and practical.

With tremendous fear and trepidation I registered for two general education requirements in the fall. I had never been so afraid in my life. (And I'm counting car accidents and riots in South Africa.) I can see now that I was scared to death because I was taking a major risk. I was putting this vision, this dream, myself in fact, on the line—could I learn and grow again?

And oh how I loved history and philosophy. I felt like leaves in the spring; just when you thought that all the trees and shrubs had died in the winter, out they come—fresh, wrinkly, incorrigible. Everything I learned connected to all that I had ever learned.

But along with history and philosophy, as an elementary education major I had to do twenty hours of experience in the classroom. I arranged to go to my children's school, to join a favorite teacher and her class of twenty second-graders. That was a great moment—my future vocation!

I lasted about two hours. I couldn't stand it! (I have the deepest respect for people who teach elementary school. They are living proof to me that God gives different people different gifts and callings, and I thank God for that.) I left second grade, shattered. My dreams, my future as I'd planned it . . . gone.

My husband was a little surprised. We had planned to pay back the student loans when I got one of those thousands of elementary education jobs. "Is there anything else you'd like to major in?" he asked.

"Oh, yes," I answered. "English literature or writing or philosophy or history or theology. But a job . . ."

I went to the career counseling office, and I got a much better understanding of my gifts and abilities. Then I did informational interviews. It became clear that what would really suit me would be to become a college professor and a writer. Fantastic.

But, of course, impossible. There were no jobs. No one makes money as a writer, and there were few college teaching positions available.

The career counselor suggested I should take my quandary to a real counselor, a psychological counselor. I told her my dilemma—this shattered dream—and she and I sat in her office and cried. Cried at the impossibility of it. Cried that a person could get so excited about something that was absolutely impossible.

What I hadn't noticed was that I had passed a turning point. I had been given, or found or perhaps claimed, myself. Somehow by taking classes and writing papers and meeting new people I had been given this self who was not somebody's wife, somebody's mom, somebody's daughter. I had discovered a sense of identity. I was a person who was called.

My journey was not all easy. As I began to know this new self, I became unwilling to be molded by others. Those who wanted me to be someone else. Those who thought I should just be practical for heaven's sake. Others who wanted me to be back in my old form— who thought I would mess up my marriage and my kids if I didn't always put them first. My husband was not one of these; he didn't seem to miss the helpmeet and minister's wife he'd lost. And he knew the Scriptures well enough to know that I needed to find my own way of following Jesus and using my gifts.

So there I was with a self and a calling. With the encouragement of many people, I decided that I could do nothing other than pursue the dream. It was risky. Scary. It was a major act of faith, something I couldn't have imagined doing a few months before.

For me to decide to go back to school, to study and find a way of following and serving Jesus outside the home, was a major risk. To do it I had to admit that I hadn't arrived, that I needed to keep growing.

Don't get me wrong. I recognize my years as full-time mother and homemaker as a remarkable privilege. I loved being able to read to my children for hours; I fully enjoyed days wandering through the botanical garden or playing on the beach.

Yet this loss of self that I had experienced—is it a necessary part of being a full-time mother for a number of years? Not necessarily.

What I was missing (perhaps because of marrying young, or fundamentalist influence, or the extremely conservative South African society) was a sense of myself as a person who was gifted and called. Lacking that, it was easy for me to completely lose myself in mothering and homemaking, to completely lose a vision for my life.

I know women who keep the vision alive, who pursue the dream as they raise young children. They work part time, pursue new skills; they take classes or learn to sculpt; they invest themselves in demanding volunteer work. In essence, they use their time home with young children as a kind of sabbatical to enrich themselves, check priorities, rethink callings and plan new ways to pursue them.

But it's tough to keep the dream alive. I have often wondered why it's so difficult. Motherhood's demands are constant; how can a person concentrate when her nights are broken and every thought interrupted? When my children were small, I didn't have enough self-respect to claim my own time or to find a room with a lock on the door in which to pursue a calling.

Yes, motherhood is tough, but what makes it tougher is that our culture doesn't value mothering. Our culture deeply respects money, qualifications and important people, and it despises choices that don't bring in bundles, don't result in a list of initials after a name, don't put a person in touch with the movers and shakers. Even those who disagree with our culture's valuing believe it at some level. Think of how we speak in hushed tones about people with certain kinds of jobs, qualifications, connections. Think of how the Christian subculture elevates those who are rich, well-known, well-connected.

In a local magazine, a woman wrote a column defending full-time motherhood, signing her name with her qualifications as a lawyer. On one level (the article itself) she was arguing that motherhood is important; on a deeper level (her statement of who she is) she was agreeing with the culture. What makes her really important, what makes her any kind of authority on anything (even motherhood), is a law degree—the fact that she could be making big bucks, that she has legal qualifications and that she probably knows important people.

Most women struggle not to lose themselves in the demands of mothering, the boredom of housework and our culture's devaluation of anything that doesn't make money. They lose a sense of self-esteem, a sense of themselves as gifted and called.

I am not the sort of person who cries easily. But when I think of what my life would have been like if I had not had the nerve to go back to school, I start to cry. How would I feel now if I hadn't found my own identity outside my husband and children, if I'd not pursued a dream, if I'd not found a sense of my own gifts and calling, if I'd not decided to follow Jesus on my own path of discipleship? The regret would have hurt, it would have grown like a cancer, it would have turned into helpless rage, carefully masked with a polite smile.

To keep balanced and growing, I had to find Jesus' call to me. I had to learn to discern the false voices that were offering me easy answers but would pull me off balance.

The Power of the False Voices

When people ask me about my decision to go back to school and pursue my calling, I tell them how terrified I was to take that first college class. I tell them that I didn't believe I could pass a class. Often men will say to me, "Are you kidding?"

Women know I'm not kidding. Many of them know what it's like to lose themselves and to have little sense of themselves as gifted and called. They know what it's like to have completely forgotten that there is a place where their "deep gladness and the world's deep hunger meet."

Jesus' voice, calling me to keep following, had been swept away. What had replaced it? False voices.

It's hard for any of us to discern where this clamor of voices comes from. But these voices echo through our culture until we assume that they tell things as they are, much as people assumed that slavery was just a fact of life.

Women easily weave onto their warp whatever seems to come to hand without questioning it. In fact we need to carefully examine the materials we accept, see where they come from and reject them if necessary. We want to follow the call of Jesus, not some other call that claims to be his.

Many of the voices wooing women sound very good, but what they offer moves a woman out of her essential balance and focus on Christ, encouraging her to spin off-balance in her life. Let's look at these voices.

3
Saying No
to Superwoman

*W*omen want to follow Christ, but a woman's life is a complicated montage of color, texture and pattern, pieced together from her identity, her calling and her work. Women want their lives to be a balanced work of art in which they accomplish goals, but within a network of relationships.

Literally thousands of voices tell women what they should do with their lives. From the self-help books that suggest she find herself, dump all other commitments and dance with the goddess to the radio preachers who tell her that homemaking and motherhood are all the calling she'll ever need, and a hundred other voices in between—there's no shortage of those who would tell women how to live.

Those who don't understand how a woman could lose herself and her calling don't recognize the strength of these false voices.

The Call to Be Superwoman

For fifteen years Lucy climbed the ladders of corporate America. She worked for Honeywell, and although others fell by the wayside, she became a manager and then a director. Raised in a very conservative, fear-filled home, she found that her work gave her something she really wanted—a way to see herself as successful, a stimulating way to spend her days (and often evenings), the impressed glances of others and a nice big paycheck. She often dated but wasn't married, and she enjoyed her job.

Recalling these years later, she saw the beginning of her dissatisfaction some years earlier. She was called into her boss's office and told that a fellow manager was losing his job. The boss hadn't told the man; he wanted Lucy to let him know. She saw her coworker's devastation and began to wonder why she was working as hard as she was for someone as amoral as her boss.

Then Lucy married and was transferred to Australia, where the company kept her and her husband in high style. She was beginning to notice how many of her coworkers were driven by ambition, their whole lives being totally poured out in their work. Although she saw this clearly in other people, she still enjoyed her own work and didn't mind the sacrifices she was making.

One afternoon in her office in Sydney, Lucy passed out. The next day she again passed out. Medical tests showed nothing, and Lucy was sent to see a counselor. The counselor told her that in his years of counseling corporate executives, he'd seen that women often gave more of themselves to their work until they burned out. He suggested that she cut back.

So Lucy decided to come back to the United States and give up her directorship. "It was one of the hardest things I've done. I was afraid people would think I couldn't cope, that I had never really deserved to be a director. That I was an inadequate person. It was hard to tell people about my decision."

A couple of years later, Lucy was still feeling dissatisfied. Corporate cutbacks meant that she was working longer and longer hours. She tried not to bring work home, so she stayed later and later.

One day she decided to take a week off, just to see what it was like. "I'd never taken a week off without traveling or doing a project. I wondered how I'd like it. During that week, I decided to quit.

"What I realized was that I was giving my life—throwing it away, really—to something that, although I had once found it stimulating intellectually, I wasn't sure I wanted to give my life to. I wondered if what I was doing was really important. I don't want to say this means that other people might not be called to be there. But I had begun to see that I wasn't."

Some people, she said, seemed jealous that she was quitting. Others seemed to imply that she was selling out. What was Lucy selling out of? The dream of the superwoman. "I realized that the fact that I could do this job and do it well didn't mean that I had to do it."

Lucy is unsure about her future plans, and right now she doesn't need to know. She is aware that she's fortunate to be able to afford financially to make this kind of decision. She wants to spend some time getting in touch with what she really wants to do and where her gifts lie. Her future work might be paid or not.

The Women's Movement and the Superwoman

Lucy found freedom to ignore the voice that was telling her, "Be a superwoman; you can do it!" She simply said no. A hundred years ago, however, women would not have had Lucy's choices. The women's movement has expanded women's choices enormously.

We should be thankful for the gifts the women's movement has given us. Which of us would want to go back to the days when boys were encouraged to be boys, and girls paid the price? How about the days when women couldn't give evidence in a court of law? Which of us would want to go back to a time when sexual harassment in the workplace, the university, college or school was the norm? How about the days when a woman's voting rights were considered a threat to the American family? How about the days when women were turned down for many university programs simply because they were women?

As Mary Stewart Van Leeuwen points out in a *Christianity Today* review,[1] there are many benefits of feminism which conservative Christians gratefully accept even as they listen to people labeling feminists as witches and "feminazis." We all need to thank God for the women who were willing to be arrested if that got them closer to getting the vote, for the women who protested and worked so that research money began to be funneled toward studies of breast cancer and other women's diseases, for the women who campaigned so that our daughters needn't fear that they will be asked to exchange sexual favors for grades in college.

Not only can we choose to vote, choose not to wear high heels and choose to get an education, but women can now choose to take the track blazed by men toward total life dedication to the corporate dream. In many ways women's lives have been enriched, but many would agree that our lives are more complex because of the many choices we now face.

The Unbalanced Male Dream

It's been several decades now since the voices started telling women that they could "have it all." There was a time when women believed and tried it. They saw themselves moving up through the ranks. They enjoyed being the first woman head of this and first woman member on the board of that.

These women were highly motivated. Many had seen what happened to their own mothers, who had found all their financial security in marriage as their fathers made enough money to support the family. But they saw the mom become more and more manipulative. Or the dad get tired of being the sole breadwinner, enslaved to his work, and take off with a "cute" new wife. Women who were untrained for anything were unable to support themselves.[2]

Gradually women who listened to voices telling them to become superwomen came to realize that their quality of life was suffering. Word got around that they were exhausted and unable to cope with demands of high-powered jobs, mothering children and keeping a marriage intact. The unmarried began to see that their jobs were demanding their very souls and keeping them from healthy relationships. And things have only gotten worse.

Experts claim that these are days of unprecedented workaholism and burnout. We've all met the victims, people who are working fifty-five- and sixty-hour weeks but who still feel that they are never caught up with their work. Middle-management labor cuts leave thousands wondering what their lives are about.

The voice calling women to become superwomen is a false voice that tells women not to be themselves but to be like men, adopting the same standards of success. It can be heady to answer the question "What do you do?" in terms of a high-powered job. But some women who opted for a career path hoping it would bring fulfillment instead find themselves feeling empty and exhausted. They realize that they have bought into the lie that career or financial success brings happiness and fulfillment. As psychologist Mary Mason points out, "Many women who had found their voices moved into male-dominated professions and then took on the voice of the 'male baritone.' " In other words, what seemed like wonderful new opportunities for women were in fact an opportunity for women to play men's games by men's rules.[3]

Most of us have met women who made choices because of the call to be superwoman—for example, a woman who really wanted to teach children but felt that she ought to become a lawyer. Or we have met women who have "made it" in a traditionally male-dominated sphere, like the academic world, but have paid an astronomical price, such as trading in their compassion for tenure.

The superwoman syndrome has pushed women into "stress, exhaustion, conflict, guilt, resentment and feelings of deprivation of maternal privileges, far more often than it results in the feelings of freedom and fulfillment for which it was designed."[4] No man or woman should work a sixty-hour week, giving their life to a company, although many have often done that.

Wilma had been a high-powered corporate lawyer for years and then stayed home when her children were small. When she went back to work in a similar job, she found that she was adding another shift. She would pick up the children and come home to cook a meal and organize laundry. When her husband got home from his similar job, she would go out and do grocery shopping and errands. Even when she hired a nanny, it didn't really help. "There's some stuff only I can do," she said. "And besides, I want us to be around our children. And this hasn't done any wonders for our marriage. We hardly see each other at all." Many women who have seized the new opportunities agree. Exhausted by the pressures on them, they find that they cannot be superwomen, at least not for long.

More choices have been difficult for women, according to Sylvia Ann Hewlett in her book *A Lesser Life*. Women find themselves combining two full-time jobs—total dedication to corporate life, like Wilma and Lucy experienced, and a fifties model of mothering.[5] Both are complete and total jobs, both arguably sick distortions of a balanced life.

Superwoman Is Dead

Women face choices at every turn about how they will live their lives, and these choices can seem almost overwhelming. The call to be superwoman, in its own right, is the call to follow a male paradigm, to put work and career before all else. The superwoman is dead, according to many contemporary women, because the losses involved in trying to do it all are too great.

Women don't want to be men. Relationships are important to women, and they don't want to build lives in which family and friends take last place while their careers thrive. The call to be a superwoman is a false call.

But what are our alternatives?

Most women, unfortunately, have a ready alternative. Lurking in our minds, always ready to leap on center stage, is a powerful image of what a *really* good woman is like. This image of the *really* good woman is more powerful to most of us than the superwoman, and deserves our close examination. Whether we wake or sleep, this notion of the perfect woman hangs over our heads.

4
Saying No to the Domestic Angel

*W*hat is a *really good* woman like? For a number of years I have started women's seminars by asking small groups to answer this question. I suggest that they ponder their upbringing—books they've read, movies and sitcoms they've watched, cartoons and advertisements to which they've been exposed. Then I ask them to write a list of at least twenty qualities of this really good woman. (You might try this on your own right now.)

This exercise is a snap. Within five minutes, women have made long lists. But what surprises me is the uniformity of these lists. I've asked this question in groups of women at small, radical liberal arts colleges, gatherings of older women in Baptist churches, and other groups of women of all ages and denominations—Lutherans, Episcopalians, Pentecostals, Presbyterians, Catholics—and the lists are almost identical. Where do our ideas of the perfect woman come from?

This woman is so familiar to us that we assume her to be the paradigm of perfection. Surely she must lead the perfect, balanced life.

Allow me to introduce you to this perfect woman, drawn from what women have listed at many talks and seminars. I'm sure you'll recognize her.

We've all seen her: the perfect woman.

She seems to always wear a dress or skirt (or a smart pantsuit), and her colors are perfect. (She knows her color season!)

Her children are clean and neatly dressed.

She irons for herself and the family, and she washes the family sheets once a week.

She bakes for her kids' lunches and for after-school snacks. The smell of dinner is usually wafting around an hour or so before hubby comes in. Often concerned that there might not be enough, she cooks more than she needs to. After everyone is seated, she keeps scurrying around, making sure everyone has what they need.

She's the one who is usually waiting to pick up the kids in the van after school. But if she's not the chauffeur, she prefers to ride in back.

She scouts out great bargains, getting items 50 percent off or buying clothes inexpensively because she's willing to make minor repairs.

On holidays she runs here and there buying presents, worrying if he will like this or if she would prefer a different color. She wonders if she will get her knitting project done by Christmas Eve. Why didn't she get the Christmas cookies done in time? The cards—oh dear, they might get out a few days late.

She keeps up on the family correspondence. She writes to her husband's family as well as her own, and is in charge of inviting people over for dinner.

She worries quite a lot about her weight. It would be bad if she put on too much and became unattractive to her husband. She exercises a bit to keep her weight down.

She hates keeping people waiting. For her the feeling of causing even the smallest inconvenience for someone is very hard. She apologizes a lot, as if even her existence is a nuisance. "I'm sorry," she says.

"Excuse me." "I seem to be in the way." "Can you see okay?"

It's hard for her to discuss things because she is distracted by the bitty material of her life—the driving, the phone calls, the car pools, the groceries, the ironing, the dry-cleaning, the laundry, the errands, the endless petty demands.

She is very sweet. She tries not to lose her temper.

Just under the sweet exterior is an air of anxiety, of distraction. Where did I put that recipe? Where should I buy the pork chops? What if Joey has forgotten his homework? Should I serve the salad before the main course or with it?

The perfect woman: how can she be everywhere at once—in different denominations, in different parts of the country, in all strata of society, in both urban and rural communities? How does she do it?

If this perfect woman came from biblical teaching or some other wonderfully respected authority, it would be easier to understand the similarity of our images of her and her power over us.

We all drank our ideas of this good woman with our mother's milk. We ingested her in television programs, movies, books, cartoons, magazines, advertisements. The perfect woman haunts us; we all carry some piece of her within us. Because her voice echoes so strongly in our ears, we need to understand her and also know where she hails from.

You'd almost think, from the way people talk, that this mythic woman was part of the prelapsarian state in the Garden of Eden. Or that her job description was handed down as the eleventh commandment. Or that she is praised in some alternative version of Proverbs 31. In fact the idea harks all the way back to the Victorian era.

Before the Perfect Woman

To understand the perfect domestic angel, we need to look at ideas of men and women and work before she arrived on the scene. Before the industrial revolution, all work was centered on the household, where men and women worked and goods were consumed and produced. Into the eighteenth century, women's and men's hard work was associated with godliness and salvation, and there was plenty of work to be done, according to British writer Dorothy L. Sayers. This is what women did in the Middle Ages:

It is a formidable list of jobs: the whole of the spinning industry, the whole of the dyeing industry, the whole of the weaving industry. The whole catering industry and . . . the whole of the nation's brewing and distilling. All the preserving, pickling and bottling industry, all the bacon-curing. And (since in those days a man was often absent from home for months together on war or business) a very large share in the management of landed estates.[1]

In colonial America the strong, capable women who worked beside men were called yoke-mates or meet helps. Women and men worked hard, usually together, to survive and build lives for themselves and their families.

But in the nineteenth century women came to be referred to as dependents; it was in 1840 that the term *breadwinner* was first coined for the husband.[2] A tremendous paradigm shift had occurred in understandings of women and their work. What happened to bring about this change in attitude toward women's work and roles?

The Opposite Sex
We know that the industrial revolution brought about tremendous changes in terms of lifestyle and technology in Europe and North America. But one of the most extraordinary outcomes in Britain was the rise of the middle class. Wealthy business owners and bureaucrats became almost indistinguishable from the aristocracy, at least in terms of money and possessions. This mobility, in a society long characterized by rigid class distinctions, brought about a deep anxiety, which experts argue is crucial to understanding Victorian culture.[3] Historians believe that in the anxiety wrought by class fluidity, society needed an anchor for its soul, and this anchor became the home.[4]

Instead of the home being a place where you ate and worked and slept and lived, the home began to be characterized as a haven. And in this haven, one person truly belonged, and that was the wife.

We're used to the idea of male and female as opposite, but this idea was new in Victorian England, where men and women came to be seen as polar opposites, functioning in completely separate spheres—hers the home and his the working world. The idea of "opposite sexes" seems almost biblical to us, but it's not. (I try to imagine Adam in the Garden of Eden. Instead of saying, "Now this is bone of my bones and flesh of my flesh," he might say, "Oh my gosh, my complete opposite—she's tender where I'm tough; she's pure where I'm a guy; she love kids and I'm into pruning trees!") Now we would all agree that the sexes are different, but the idea of them as opposite—this is pure Victorian invention.

The man came to be seen as the tough, aggressive, self-made, competitive creature who lived in one sphere—the rough-and-tumble of the world where he fought for a living for his sheltered family.[5] The perfect woman who stayed within her home was the opposite of her man: her highest womanly virtues were inversions of male traits. The more he was a competitive aggressor, the more she was motherly and self-sacrificing; the more he was a sexual brute, the more she was divinely pure. During the years when this ideal was being developed, characteristics that had earlier been regarded as dangerous vices in women—such as vanity, indecisiveness, laziness and silliness—were encouraged as the true nature of women.[6]

In this ideal, formed within Victorian society, the more separate the spheres in which man and woman functioned—the more opposite they were—the better. A Victorian man had "arrived" if his wife and daughters could sit idly at home, radiating moral superiority; they would not even do any housework, cook or look after children, since these all dirtied their hands. This ideal was achieved only by a few, but it was a standard to which much of society aspired. People used the new Darwinian science to suggest that women's gentleness, kindness and intuitive approaches actually sprang from male and female biology.[7]

The Angel in the House
The idea of this perfect woman was popularized in a poem by Cov-

entry Patmore called "The Angel in the House,"[8] which was passed around in cards and stitched into wall hangings. But much of the thinking about men and women functioning in completely separate spheres was hammered out in John Ruskin's very popular essay "Of Queen's Gardens." This essay was much circulated, read, discussed and believed. It's hard for us to imagine its effect. Perhaps like the movie *Schindler's List* or books like Rachel Carson's *Silent Spring* or George Orwell's *1984*, "Of Queen's Gardens" affected the way people thought about their world, further reinforcing ideas about the domestic angel and the separate spheres.

Ruskin wrote,

> The man's power is active, progressive, defensive. He is eminently the doer, the creator, the discoverer, the defender. His intellect is for speculation and invention. . . . But the woman's power is not for rule, not for battle,—and her intellect is not for invention or creation, but for sweet ordering, arrangement, and decision. . . . Her great function is Praise.[9]

This domestic angel, despite her gentleness and motherliness, has wonderful power to influence man, making him more noble by her influence. It became the woman's task to lead their children into moral superiority; only a woman could do this, because she was morally superior. Ruskin extols the virtues of the home:

> This is the true nature of home—it is a place of Peace. . . . And wherever a true wife comes, this home is always round her. . . . To fulfill this, she must . . . be incapable of error. . . . She must be enduringly, incorruptibly good; instinctively, infallibly wise—wise, not for self-development, but for self-renunciation.[10]

According to Ruskin, not only do women have responsibility for establishing this kind of home, but they are solely responsible for its failure. If something is wrong in the home (or even society), it is the fault of the woman: hers is the moral authority. Ruskin adds:

> There is not a war in the world, no, nor an injustice, but you women are answerable for it; not in that you have provoked, but in that you have not hindered. . . . There is no suffering, no injustice, no

misery in the earth, but the guilt of it lies with you—Men can bear the sight of it, but you should not be able to bear it.[11]

God, the Victorians believed and Ruskin taught, had divinely ordained this wonderful symbiosis between man and woman as she provided a haven for him (physically and morally) and he protected and provided for her; and God had formed men and women with inherently different natures so that they would fit perfectly into these roles. And so the domestic angel, developed by the Victorians and especially popularized by John Ruskin, became the ideal in England.[12]

On the American frontier, women's work was simply too important for them to be relegated to an ornamental role like their European sisters.[13] But around the time of the Civil War, the ideal of the domestic angel (also known as the Cult of True Womanhood) was imported from England. Women were told that they should quit their jobs (taken to help the war effort) or else the whole fabric of society would fall apart.

The Domestic Angel's Effect on Society

Ruskin's dream became the middle-class ideal for decades. If a middle-class woman was forced to work for financial reasons, she would lose her status as a lady.[14] Justifications for keeping men and women in completely separate spheres abounded: "The only way to make husbands sober and industrious is to keep women dependent by means of insufficient wages," wrote a *New York Post* writer.[15] Men, told that to be a good man they must support their family single-handedly, worked longer and longer hours, until they had little time with their families.

An unmarried woman was stranded in a desperate situation by this Victorian ideal. Not only was she unable to fulfill woman's highest calling, marriage, but she was also unable to take up meaningful work and still be accepted as a good woman. In this way the spinster was so outside the mainstream of society that she became a source of mirth.

Of course the Ruskin ideal was only a distant dream for the poor.

In the late nineteenth and early twentieth centuries most families couldn't manage on one income, so daughters or sons were sent out to find some sort of work—cleaning or laundering. Often families took in boarders.[16] No one showed much concern for those who were too poor to not work, as Sayers points out:

> There has never been any question but that the women of the poor should toil alongside their men. No angry, and no compassionate, voice has been raised to say that women should not break their backs with harvest work, or soil their hands with blacking grates and peeling potatoes. The objection is only to work that is pleasant, exciting or profitable—the work that any human being might think it worth while to do.[17]

We may marvel that some piece of popular culture could wield such a strong influence. The domestic angel, developed in the industrial revolution and made famous by John Ruskin and Victorian culture, was an ideal that few attained, except during the 1950s and 1960s.

The Domestic Angel in the Fifties

Contrary to popular opinion, the decade of the fifties was "not the last gasp of the traditional family life with deep roots in the past. Rather, it was the first wholehearted effort to create a home that would fulfill virtually all its members' personal needs."[18] The fifties and early sixties in the West were the only time in the history of the world when the "traditional family" ever existed in vast numbers, the only time when the domestic angel was widely esteemed and emulated, when the practice of one spouse working outside and the other in the home was widespread.

In fact the family life of the fifties was based on a historical fluke, on a certain conjunction of economic, social and political factors. People had had the opportunity to save money during World War II. Then came the postwar boom and government help for education and home ownership. During the fifties, real wages increased by more than they had in the entire previous half-century.

The fifties were singular in many ways. For women of this period the pressure was terrible. The good Victorian woman had had servants to help her, and the good mother of the 1920s and 1930s had filled a role that had finite limits: she provided wholesome food, hygienic surroundings and lots of discipline. But the role of the good mother of the fifties knew no bounds. In addition to their other duties, these mothers became personally responsible for the psychological and cognitive development of their children.[19] Mothers in this period were told that motherhood should be their whole life, and yet they were also told that anything that might go wrong with their children—depression or schizophrenia or homosexuality—was all their fault.[20]

The Ideal Begins to Slide

Images of *Leave It to Beaver* and *Father Knows Best* stick in our minds, glorifying those wonderful days. Father was out in the big, bad world doing his work—work that was demanding and quite mysterious to the rest of the family. The mother was always dressed beautifully, with an apron of course, and had the right stuff baking and cooking. She got the laundry and housework done and never seemed to struggle over her priorities.[21]

Yes, we saw it all in sitcoms, but the domestic goddess also pervaded magazines. Here's part of a *Time* article from the fifties praising the suburban housewife, the keeper of the American Dream:

> In the absence of her commuting, city-working husband, she is first of all the manager of home and brood and beyond that a sort of apronned activist. . . . With children on her mind and under her foot, she is breakfast-getter, laundress, house cleaner, dishwasher, shopper, gardener, encyclopedia, arbitrator of children's disputes [and] policeman. If she is not pregnant, she wonders if she is. She takes her peanut-butter sandwich lunch while standing, thinks she looks a fright, watches her weight (periodically) and jabbers over the short-distance telephone with her next-door neighbor.[22]

Magazines portrayed the happy woman and the happy family, and they roundly condemned women who worked outside the home. Here's an excerpt from *Look* magazine in 1956:

The American woman is winning the battle of the sexes. Like a teenager, she is growing up and confounding her critics. . . . She works, rather casually, less towards a big career than as a way of filling a hope chest or buying a home freezer. She gracefully concedes the top jobs to men. This wondrous creature also marries younger than ever, bears more babies and looks and acts far more feminine than the "emancipated" girl of the 1920s or even 30s. Steel worker's wife and Junior Leaguer alike do their own housework.[23]

It's little wonder that when Betty Friedan's *The Feminine Mystique* was published in 1962 it caused such an outcry. Friedan wondered why women who seemingly had it all—a man, children, a house and even certain laborsaving devices like washing machines—were suffering from a "gnawing inner malaise."[24] She called it "the problem that has no name" and saw that it drove record numbers of women to tranquilizer use and drug and alcohol abuse, and into general boredom and depression. Tranquilizer use, almost unheard of in 1955, reached 462,000 pounds in 1958 and 1.15 million pounds a year later.[25] Women were not even able to ask the question, Is this all?

The Victorian ideal of women relied on an air of mystery, a mystique surrounding their sex: they needed to be so entirely other than men that they could hardly be understood. They needed to be pure and happy with small, domestic things. This mystique about women reached its zenith in the fifties. Sayers writes this of the mystique:

> There is no special mystery about women, except what men have manufactured to feed their own vanity; a woman is a person and a fellow creature, and the sort of "love" which is founded on a refusal to face this fact is a delusion and a wrong. Jesus made no foolish mysteries about women, He treated them just like anybody else—as persons. He is the only religious teacher who has ever been quite sane on this point—almost, I was going to say, the only man. But, having made women, presumably, He knew what they were like.[26]

Women's otherness from men, their purer, kinder, gentler nature—this was the "mystery" that made it possible for women to be put on pedestals as domestic angels. After five years of writing, research and interviews, Friedan reached the conclusion that the mystique of the feminine "permits, even encourages, women to ignore the question of their identity. The mystique says that they can answer the question 'Who am I?' by saying 'Tom's wife . . . Mary's mother . . .' "[27] Women were allowed by this mystique to stop growing, not to be interested in the life of the mind. She found women whose housework expanded to fill time; with the addition of another laborsaving device, women found the freedom to wash the sheets twice rather than once a week.

The happy housewife was the predominant image of women on television and in magazines, but Friedan, in all her interviews, found none. She would follow leads, thinking, *At last, a happy housewife!* and then find that the woman was depressed or had attempted suicide or was abusing alcohol.

In many ways the power of the domestic angel has been broken. What appeared to be a wonderfully balanced person turned out to be someone who was out of kilter and deeply unhappy. Once she was seen to be human and not some mysterious other, she lost her power. In fact she was found to never have existed.

But although no one reads Ruskin's "On Queen's Gardens" much anymore, the domestic angel still haunts us. Although few aspire to be her, we all carry some piece of her within us.

Christian women find themselves in the most difficult position. On the one hand, the women's movement has proclaimed a gospel that seeks to liberate women by calling them to be superwomen. On the other hand, Christian preachers and teachers have encouraged women to stand fast and cling to the gospel according to John Ruskin.

5
Saying No
to the Christian
Domestic Angel

C hristian women are bombarded by many voices telling them
how to live their lives. But the most dreadful and seductive voice
is the subtlest one of all. Echoing as it does many of the cultural
messages we were raised with, this voice sounds so right somehow. It
is the voice that tells a woman to be a Christian domestic angel. But
it owes much more to Ruskin than it does to Jesus.

Ruskin or Jesus?
Natalie came into my office. "I need to talk," she said. She dropped
her bag and collapsed into a chair. "I don't think I can do it. I'd
counted on the schoolwork, the papers and reading, and I'm absolutely loving that. But what I hadn't figured on was the adjustment the
family would have to make. They're finding it tough. All those after-
school cookie-baking sessions with my daughter. Yesterday when I got

out the store-bought cookies again—and I got there about half an hour after she did—she groaned at me. Told me she wanted her old mom back." Tears came into Natalie's eyes.

"Then my son's schoolwork has gone downhill. The teacher says it's probably just an adjustment period, or maybe he's acting out, seeing what kind of response he'll get, but I'm upset. He was a really gifted student.

"And my husband. Wednesday of this week, he went to bed on his own. I had papers to finish. We've never done that. Not in fifteen years of married life. And the house is chaos. I haven't washed the sheets in almost a month. So I think I should quit school. Though I'd always promised myself I'd go back . . ."

I handed her a Kleenex and shook my head. I knew her predicament very well. I'd gone back to finish a degree ten years before, and I remembered the adjustment period. (Especially the day that my daughter Susannah was pretending to read a picture page from Sunday school and I overheard her saying, "And then the blind man said to Jesus, 'Jesus, please help me!' And Jesus said to him, 'Leave me alone, can't you see I'm trying to write a paper?' ")

"It is a hard adjustment for everyone," I said. "But what makes you say maybe you should quit?"

"My sister-in-law and my neighbor. They both go to the Bible study I used to go to, and they said that they felt maybe I was neglecting my God-given calling. And I know it's true. My highest calling is to be a wife and mother and homemaker, and if I can't do those as well, then maybe I should quit."

Another Kleenex. We sat silently for a few minutes.

"But who's telling them that? Who's telling you that? Do you see what I'm saying? What makes you think that baking cookies with your daughter and washing sheets is as important as developing your gifts and using them for Jesus?"

She looked at me blankly. "Everyone knows that. I've heard it on the radio, at church—"

"Listen. Do me a favor. Before you make a decision, see what Jesus says about it. Read one of the Gospels, maybe Luke or Matthew, and see which Jesus wants you to do. Look at the way he calls the women, what he expects them to do. Okay?"

Natalie was back, clutching her Bible, a week later. "It's amazing. You know, I've been to so many Bible studies it would make your head swim, but . . . Jesus didn't tell the women to bake cookies. Besides the bit where Peter's mother-in-law serves them, after being healed, there's nothing like that. Martha gets told to get her priorities right, to stop being so domestic and start spending time like any other disciple with her teacher. And all the way through, Jesus calls the women to be disciples, to follow, just like the men. And the women were the ones who followed him, right to the cross, the burial and the tomb."

She pulled a piece of paper out of her Bible. "Why haven't I seen this before? In fact, if anything Jesus seems to play down family." She closed her Bible. "And that's only one Gospel. What's odd is that I realize now that some of this stuff didn't make sense to me, but I didn't know why. And when I started back to school, it felt so good, but I practically thought I ought to feel guilty."

Natalie sat down. "Okay. What I want to know is this: how have I been given the impression that to be a really good Christian woman has less to do with becoming a follower of Jesus and more to do with keeping my house dusted and my husband in ironed shirts? Where have I gotten the message that my calling as a Christian woman is to be a domestic queen rather than a disciple?"

It took me awhile to explain where the idea of the domestic angel comes from. She'd already seen that it isn't in the Bible, and I had to tell her that it owed quite a lot to John Ruskin, who elaborated on what a good woman is like in a time of great social turmoil in England, and how that idea became prevalent as an ideal to be aspired to. It was a little difficult to explain that this ideal of a domestic angel and her proper sphere only in the home was such a recent idea, and that it was only widely achieved after John Ruskin was long dead—in the fifties and sixties, when it often led to terrible depression and isolation. I added that although this ideal has been fading for some time, it exists still in the minds of certain preachers, who hold up the domestic angel myth as an ideal that women should conform to today.

Natalie laughed. "I'd rather follow Jesus Christ than John Ruskin." "Great choice," I said.

Natalie finished her degree and now teaches English as a second language in an inner-city school. She enjoys her family, and when I see her she speaks of the freedom she has found to be herself, use her gifts and witness for Jesus in a largely secular workplace.

A happy ending for Natalie. But what about the women who hear only the voices telling them that a 150-year-old ideal is God's highest design?

The Christian Domestic Angel

When I ask women to list some of the qualities of the really good woman, I used to ask them to make another list: The Good Christian Woman. But I stopped. It was really unnecessary, because the two lists were almost identical.

Christians have adopted this cultural artifact from Victorian society as the gospel truth. In so doing, the church has allowed itself to be led by culture, not the Bible. Christians have ended up in a desperate struggle, not to encourage women to follow Jesus, but to reclaim, as historian Randall Ballmer says, the "nineteenth century ideal of femininity both for themselves and for a culture."[1] The church bought— lock, stock and barrel—what was going on in the society of the time and baptized it, calling it Christian and even biblical truth. In fact the ideas that are often labeled "traditional family values" are not biblical and not Christian; many run directly counter to biblical teaching.[2] This is the most subtle voice that tries to pull Christian women off-balance.

From Meaningful Ministry to Domesticity

The church followed culture in its preaching about women's roles, but the practical application of this teaching against meaningful work and ministry for women varied from denomination to denomination. Janette Hassey, in her book *No Time for Silence,* traces attitudes toward women in many Christian denominations, where groups that for years encouraged women in preaching and teaching roles pulled back from this position in the period between the two world wars.

The great evangelist Dwight L. Moody supported women's ministries. He welcomed Frances Willard, founder and president of the Women's Christian Temperance Union, as a coworker in his evangelistic work in Boston in 1877, encouraging her to preach the gospel, suffrage and temperance.[3] Just before the turn of the century, Moody established special scholarships for gifted women at the Moody Bible Institute.[4] In fact, women dominated American Bible colleges numerically, with the largest number of graduates choosing foreign missions—a task chosen by few married or single men.[5]

The complex response of fundamentalists to the domestic angel is traced by church historian Margaret Bendroth in *Fundamentalism and Gender*. In the early days, fundamentalists reacted against sentimental ideas of women's greater purity. "By the 1920s fundamentalists had adopted the belief that it was men, not women, who had the true aptitude for religion."[6] Women were perceived as psychologically and emotionally vulnerable and therefore not to be trusted with doctrine, teaching and leadership. Instead a strong image of the "macho Christian" came to the fore—the Christian warrior doing battle against the female Babylon.[7]

Nevertheless, many evangelical women continued to be active in teaching and especially in missionary roles through the mid-1940s. Employed as field workers in student and children's organizations, at least as many fundamentalist women went along with the national trend and were employed outside the home through the 1940s.[8]

After World War II, along with society in general, attitudes toward women changed, so that their proper sphere came to be the home rather than the mission field.[9] Society as a whole was threatened by rapid social change after the war, and the fundamentalist response was a movement toward greater hierarchy and masculine control; this deeply affected male and female experience of Christian institutions, ministry and the home.[10]

Women's ministries began to be restricted to their homes or to young children within the church. "A female Bible institute graduate who in 1910 may have pastored a small church or traveled as an itinerant revivalist would by 1940 more likely serve as director of religious education."[11] Hassey devotes a chapter to the Free Church and its many women revivalist preachers, pastors and evangelists early in the twentieth century. This same church in 1983 recommended against women's ministry. Having traced many evangelical denominations and institutions, Hassey says, "As with women . . . in Christian and missionary Alliance churches, women in the Free Church could publicly minister in the 1880s in ways labeled unacceptable or unbiblical by the 1980s."[12]

By the fifties a woman was no longer a person called by God and used for his glory; she had been domesticated. As Hassey shows by looking at attitudes toward women in *Moody Monthly* magazine, a new woman emerged: "the new image of God's ideal woman—no longer the Moody Bible Institute graduate who used all her gifts for the kingdom, but the submissive, domesticated woman who knows her place."[13]

The image of the tough male as the one suitable for the manly job of ministry became dominant, according to Bendroth.[14] "Attitudes toward female vocations, especially Bible teaching, became steadily more restrictive after World War II: women's primary energy was to be spent in the home,"[15] although women could be involved in support tasks as secretaries and pastors' wives.[16] Women had meaningful ministry taken away from them, and yet they were exalted as domestic angels, as we can see in this chorus:

Praying mothers, Christian homes,
Keeping families together where they belong,
Teaching trust, respect, faith, and love,
Reverence to our God above.
With love to godly mothers,
We sing this song.[17]

Straight out of Ruskin's separate spheres, this woman is unable to function outside the home. But in the home she is pure, virtuous and closer to the divine than any man could be. As Bailey Smith, an official in the Southern Baptist Convention, writes, "The highest form of God's creation is womankind."[18] She is responsible for society's ills, writes Baptist evangelist J. C. Massee: "Since woman is the determining factor in social life, [she] must of necessity be religious or destroy the very society she creates."[19] Also under pressure to ensure her children's salvation, mothers agonized over a role that included "great responsibility and limited moral authority."[20] The husband and father was told to act as high priest in the home;[21] in fact, the fundamentalist father was much like the fundamentalist God—physically absent and expressing love mainly through sacrifice and discipline.[22]

The church obediently followed the culture in its glorification of the domestic angel in the fifties and sixties. The new evangelical movement, "for all its relative openness to secular thought, carried into its 'renaissance' an extremely conservative approach to gender roles."[23] Women's vocations and ministries dropped sharply, and their sense of calling to be homemakers rose. *His* magazine, in a 1948 issue, promoted homemaking for Christ. A woman who had given up her calling to missions to become a homemaker waxed eloquent, remarking, "It is obvious that the Scriptures portray the normal Christian woman as a homemaker."[24] Women were encouraged to end their own ministries and focus on their husbands' successes.

Although these ideas were promoted as Christian, they were actually almost identical to the ideal promoted by the broader society. The only difference was the sense of a "God-given hierarchy" in the Christian home, an order that seemed to bring a sense of security in a time of disorder.[25]

The woman portrayed in many Christian magazines and books is the direct descendant of Ruskin's domestic angel, and her charge is the same: to win man back, animal that he is, by submitting her quiet spiritual authority.[26] This woman holds tremendous power to make a good man bad and a bad man good. Marabel Morgan developed this message in her book *Total Woman*. Her answer to a troubled marriage was that a woman submit to her husband in "salad, sex, or sports."[27]

Here's a woman, described by Moody Bible teacher P. B. Fitzwater in *Woman: Her Mission, Position and Ministry* (1950): "She is physically constituted to bear children and mentally and spiritually fitted to develop and mold their lives." Men, on the other hand, being out and involved in "the affairs of state," find it "impossible . . . to nurture the children."[28] This woman, with all ministry removed, became by the mid-fifties very much like the virtuous domestic angel originally rejected by fundamentalists. Exalted on her pedestal (which is the home), virtue becomes synonymous with femininity. (Can we imagine a magazine for Christian men called *Virtue?*) Although men lack the purity and virtue of women, they must make all decisions in the family and play leadership roles in the church.

The single woman, once again, is left out. Unlike the Bible, which praises the woman who remains single for the gospel, this false gospel puts single women under terrible pressure to normalize. According to the Christian domestic angel myth, the single woman is unable to attain her highest possible calling. "In many ways God measures a woman's success by her relationship with her husband and children," writes Barbara Peil in a Dallas Theological Seminary publication *Kindred Spirit*.[29] And the woman who is following God's call to her to be single—does she get an incomplete on her evaluation?

This teaching sounds so biblical that it's hard for us to believe that it's not. In fact it runs exactly counter to the teaching of the New Testament.[30]

In order to bolster their fundamentally unbiblical teaching about women, fundamentalists made radical shifts in their interpretation of New Testament passages. They "no longer interpreted passages in 1 Timothy 2 or 1 Corinthians 14 as occasional advice for specific problems; instead, these passages gave transcultural principles for all times and places. In reaction to outside threats, many fundamentalist institutions revised their earlier views about women."[31]

Conforming Our Lives to a Victorian Antique
We can hardly blame women, who have the voices of preachers (strug-

gling desperately to keep John Ruskin's ideal alive) blaring in their ears, for being confused. Something is wrong: the voice on the radio doesn't harmonize with the voice within.

Perhaps she finds herself sinking into boredom, depression or anxiety. But there is no center ground for her. She has to stand with the conservative preachers against the dangerous feminists. The shouting gets louder and louder, and she feels more and more confused. The Christian woman stops her ears, crouches and says over and over to herself, *I am fulfilled, I am fulfilled, I am fulfilled* . . . as her life streams away from her.[32]

Unlike the call of Jesus—which was the same to men and women: to follow him and become disciples—the domestic angel myth pressures women to fashion their lives after cultural ideals, not the truth of the gospel. Jesus didn't treat women differently from men, but as Sayers points out, "His followers lost little time in remedying this odd defect in His teaching."[33] Unlike the ministry of women in the early church, where gifts and calling took precedent over gender, many Christian women are told they should reverse the biblical order, orienting their lives solely around gender.

Many women, under terrible pressure to conform to a Victorian standard, leave the Christian faith, convinced that the gospel is an instrument of manipulation. They are pushed away from Jesus by those who say they follow him. And for those who remain within the Christian faith, dreadful guilt is heaped on them if they question the status quo.

Within Jesus' individual calling to women, many may be called, at least for some period in their lives, to be full-time mothers and homemakers. But to use a cultural artifact—this Victorian antique that is actually another "gospel"—to manipulate women and steal their joy, their life and their call to discipleship is inexcusable.

Personally, I'm sick of Ruskin. Let's look instead at Jesus' call to women.

Part 2
Jesus Calls Women to Focus As We Follow Him

6
Becoming
a Mature
Disciple

Now as they went on their way, he entered a certain village, where a woman named Martha welcomed him into her home. She had a sister named Mary, who sat at the Lord's feet and listened to what he was saying. But Martha was distracted by her many tasks; so she came to him and asked, "Lord, do you not care that my sister has left me to do all the work by myself? Tell her then to help me." But the Lord answered her, "Martha, Martha, you are worried and distracted by many things; there is need of only one thing. Mary has chosen the better part, which will not be taken away from her."
LUKE 10:38-42

The good Victorian woman reached the zenith of her popularity during the 1950s and now lives on in some Christian teaching. Thank God that Luke included this vignette showing Jesus' response to the domestic angel. Let's look again at Jesus' call to Martha.

Jesus' Call to the Domestic Angel
Martha was the perfect domestic angel. She had poured out her life to make everyone comfortable and happy and well fed. She had a wonderful servant spirit. People should have really appreciated her. And everyone did: they talked about what a great cook she was, how

good she was at entertaining and how she managed her household so well. Of course she lived in a culture in which women weren't encouraged to read or discuss things or follow rabbis or study the Scriptures. So everyone thought Martha was great. They gave her a lot of praise.

Except Jesus. He told her to knock off trying to impress him and others and herself with her domestic performance and to be a disciple instead.

Jesus knew that more than anything Martha needed to find herself in God. She needed to be assured of his love so that she wouldn't feel the need to impress him by her domestic skills. Then she could stop being anxious and distracted. Focused, grounded and centered in her love relationship with Jesus, she could begin to discern God's call to her. Jesus' call to Martha was a call to say no to the childishness, idolatry and time-wasting that she assumed were womanly virtues. It was a call to say yes to the things that would bring her into balance— to move toward self-recognition, step out of roles and find her calling.

Let's imagine the response Martha would get if, instead of bringing her complaint to Jesus, she brought it to one of today's many preachers and teachers who want women to be domestic angels.

Dear Sir:

I am a housewife, and I love running a household, entertaining, etc., and everyone seems to think I'm good at it. My problem is this: my sister doesn't pull her weight. It all came to a head the other day when she was actually sitting involved in a theological discussion with an itinerant preacher. Partly, I'm concerned about her getting involved in areas which are not proper to women. But also I feel imposed upon to be working so hard. The rabbi told me that I'd be better off doing as my sister does. What do you say?

Hot and Bothered in Bethany

Dear Hot and Bothered,

How right you are to be concerned for your dear sister; she is indeed stepping out of her proper role, which can only lead down the slippery slope to greater danger. Especially as she (and I assume yourself, as well) is single and without proper headship, you cannot be too careful. My suggestion is that you lock the door whenever you see this dangerous preacher on the road. His radical ideas are an affront to all properly religious people who understand the importance of hierarchy and roles. My prayers will be with you.

The advice-dispensing spiritual leader might also suggest that Martha pass on to this misguided itinerant pastor the words of a *Way of Truth* editorial: "Those who feel that a woman is wasting her time and burying her talents in being a wife and mother in the home, are simply blinded by the 'gods' of this world."[1] Perhaps this editorial advice would help put this preacher on the right track, following in John Ruskin's steps.

We sympathize with Martha. She's doing what we've all been told is our highest calling. If Luke had been a little more sensitive to the needs of nineteenth- and twentieth-century men, perhaps he wouldn't have included this story in his Gospel. Preachers struggle with this passage, as Sayers points out:

I have never heard a sermon preached on the story of Martha and Mary that did not attempt, somehow, somewhere, to explain away its text, "Mary's, of course, was the better part—the Lord said so and we must not precisely contradict Him. But we will be careful not to despise Martha. No doubt, He approved of her too. We could not get on without her, and indeed (having paid lip-service to God's opinion) we must admit that we greatly prefer her. For Martha was doing a really feminine job, whereas Mary was just behaving like any other disciple, male or female; and that is a hard pill to swallow."[2]

Such a hard pill, in fact, that two thousand years after Jesus spoke to Martha and fifty years after Sayers wrote about it, many preachers still have not quite gotten up the nerve to swallow it.

Jesus told Martha to cut out the domestic angel stuff and become a disciple. Her main task in life was not to be a terrific hostess but to follow him. He told her that her sister (of all people, that dreamy, incompetent woman) had it right. Her sister was learning from him, engaged in theological discussions, following him as a disciple. Martha's primary calling, as well, was to sit at his feet in love and dependence.

Jesus Called Women to Become Disciples

As Natalie realized from her reading of the Gospels, Jesus' call to women was a call to follow him. The word in the Gospels used for the women who follow Jesus is the same word used for the men who follow him.

Women were called to follow Jesus. *Yeah, yeah, yeah,* we think. But consider the social pressures women faced in answering Jesus' call to follow. Respectable women in first-century Judaism and society were not to be seen in public; they couldn't speak to a man in public; they could not be taught the Torah; they could never follow a rabbi; they could not make ethical decisions without the supervision of a father or husband.[3] Even if the women didn't know better, Jesus should have known that he wasn't allowed to call women, to speak to them, to teach them, to touch and be touched by them, to eat food they had prepared, to use them as illustrations in stories. Alas, not having had the benefit of Ruskin's teaching or other twentieth-century preaching, Jesus called women to be his followers.[4]

And the women responded by following him. Women disciples followed him all over Galilee. Many of them (according to all of the Gospels[5]) made the week-long trip to be with Jesus in Jerusalem when he died, a trip that was never made without proper parental or husbandly chaperoning. They were the ones who stayed with him at the cross and saw where he was buried. They were the first witnesses to his resurrection.

Jesus called women to be his followers. His call to women and his call to men were identical. The primary call to men and women is a call to discipleship.

Jesus Calls Women to Grow Up

When Jesus calls women to follow him as disciples, he is calling them to grow up, to take responsibility for their lives. This was a new experience for the women whom Jesus called. They were legally minors, unable to witness in a court of law or make decisions about property. The first-century Jewish woman's spiritual life was really the property of the family—her access to God was through the patriarchal family system.[6] As her husband had access to God, she might bask in his glory. The woman in Jesus' time was treated very much as a child.

Jesus defied cultural norms and treated women as adults. He demanded their theological reflection and challenged women to follow him.

In some Christian circles today women are treated like these women Jesus called two thousand years ago. They are treated almost as children or minors in church meetings; they have been told that they need to put themselves under the protection and authority of a man. Jesus disagreed: he called each woman to follow him in her own right.

The woman who hears the call of Jesus to wake up and grow up, the woman who is awakened from her dream of being a domestic angel, finds that she is responsible for finding what God has called her to.

Growing up can be frightening. Many women today know the feeling of being less than grown up, the terror of facing the call to maturity. Many women have assumed that someone will look after them; they don't know what to do when the car breaks down or the furnace quits.

We don't care much for the message of Jesus. Martha was a competent cook, for heaven's sake. Why push her into trying to think about theological issues? Why demand that she have a life quest as a disciple in her own right? She was pretty happy—why force her to grow up? Because it's part of the call to follow Jesus as a full disciple.

Jesus Calls Women to Abandon Their Idols

As women respond to Jesus, not only do they hear his call to maturity, but they also hear his call to abandon their idols. These might be the traditional male idols such as money, sex, power. Or they might be things that we have been told are good and womanly like decorating, homemaking, childrearing.

The rich young man who comes to Jesus is torn; part of him wants to follow the rabbi. After all, he's kept the commandments, and here he is, seeking out Jesus to ask him what to do. Jesus, looking at him, loves him. And in loving him, Jesus tells him to do the hardest thing possible, to throw away his idol. Jesus tells him to get rid of his possessions and follow.

Jesus pushed this poor young man to recognize what was stopping him from discipleship. "Put it aside," he said. "Follow." Jesus didn't ask the rich young man for passivity and helplessness; he didn't even ask for a faith commitment. Jesus called for an active response of faith. He was asking this young man to move beyond his comfort zone, to take a major risk with his life.[7] Instead the young man chose safety, security, what his society had told him was important, not the faith quest with Jesus.

This is true for many women today.

Most idols don't appear before us as many-armed brass gods. They are disguised, often as the distractions of our lives. One recent study shows that women often consider shopping to be part of their job description, so getting a bargain becomes deeply ingrained in who they are. Was I a good person today? Yes, I spent an hour and a half at the mall and got a 35 percent discount on bedding. Yes, it only took me the whole morning to find knobs to match the bathroom wallpaper. Studies show that bored, underemployed women tend to become more fastidious with their household tasks than others.

No big deal, we may think, that these women are "majoring on the minors." But to "major on the minors" is really a form of idolatry. We elevate something to huge proportions and treat it as if our life depended on it.

Women have been encouraged to idolize their family lives. We are so used to thinking that this is acceptable, even laudable, that we forget that Jesus stood out against this kind of idolatry.

Several times in the Gospels someone tries to get Jesus to elevate motherhood and the family; Jesus confounds his listeners by refusing. Jesus points out to his own mother that her calling to be a disciple takes primacy over her job as mother. Wanting to hear Jesus praise the institution of motherhood, a woman calls out a well-known chant: "Blessed is the womb that bore you and the breasts that nursed you!" Jesus retorts immediately: "Blessed rather are those who hear the word of God and obey it" (Luke 11:27-28). When someone in a crowd tells Jesus that his mother and siblings are outside, Jesus says, "My mother and my brothers are those who hear the word of God and do it" (Luke 8:19-21).

How could Jesus be so uncompromising on what we consider to be this most holy institution? I suspect that Jesus recognized the danger of idolizing the family. "Those who deify the family, in disregard of Christ's reiterated warnings," wrote Dorothy L. Sayers, "are from the Christian point of view equally in error with those who deify sex, or power, or pleasure."8 Many of us find it easy to judge those who live for sex, power or pleasure, but to speak out about those who idolize the family, like Jesus did, is a scary thing. It is a remarkable testimony to the power of the domestic angel myth that "Bible-believing" preachers often teach a message directly counter to the message of Jesus, and no one calls them on it.

Jesus' call to women is a call to major on what is most important—discipleship; it is a call to follow him.

Jesus Calls Women to Value Their Time

Women are called to follow Jesus, just as men are called to follow him. Women are called to use their time wisely, just as men are. There's no differentiation based on gender in the scene at Bethany—as if busy domestic frittering were fine for Martha because she's female. No, Jesus is clear that Mary has chosen the better part and Martha should choose it too. That's what disciples do.

This means we must defy the way the "world" values time. The "world" thinks that time spent in prayers and silent communion with God is time wasted. Time spent pursuing Christian growth is wasted. But Jesus in his call to Martha and his affirmation of Mary countered this: time spent in touch with him, growing in faith, is of crucial importance.

The world tells us that our most important time is time spent earning money. Women tend to earn less money, so their time is worth less than men's time, a valuation that does not come from God but from the world. All disciples are to "make the most of the time" (Ephesians 5:16).

My husband answered the phone while I was writing. It was someone from my children's school, wanting to talk to me, so he handed me the phone. "We really need help on a phone call campaign to get more people out to the Sweetheart Dinner. I wonder if you could help by phoning fifteen people."

"I'm very busy at the moment. With my teaching schedule and a couple of book deadlines, I'm afraid I don't have the time. My husband might have time—"

"Oh, no, I'm sure he's far too busy. I could never ask him. Never mind," she said as she hung up.

Her assumption, without knowing either of us at all, is that his time is inherently more valuable than mine.

These assumptions about the value of men and women's time run so deep that my husband and I realize that we have to consciously counter them all the time. Otherwise we and others assume that his time and calling are more valuable than mine.

My husband (thank the Lord) likes grocery shopping, so that is one of his areas of responsibility in our common life. One summer day he was in our local supermarket buying some supplies for dinner, and he ran into a church member. She was clearly shocked to see him there. "You . . . grocery shopping!" she said.

Ernie smiled at her and commented on how busy the store was.

"My husband wouldn't be caught dead in the grocery store. You really are a saint."

I chuckled when Ernie told me. What a wonderful double standard. To become a saint, a woman has to live her whole life with the destitute, or perhaps be put on the rack or maybe be run through with swords. To become a saint, a man has to go grocery shopping or perhaps clean a toilet.

To assume the biblical stance that all are called equally to follow God, to use their time and talents for him and to exercise their callings based on gifts, we have to fight a wealth of cultural biases that tell women their time is cheap and their callings trivial.[9] When a woman begins to sense herself as called by Jesus, she may begin to claim the time to do what she needs to do. It may be time spent in prayer, in caring for a dying parent, in writing, in going to medical school.

For a woman to claim time on her own—uninterrupted time—can be very difficult. A friend of mine was turning forty, and her husband asked her what she would like for her birthday—a Caribbean trip or a new sofa? "Oh, please," she said. "Please, please . . . I'd love four Saturdays of uninterrupted time. When you'd have the baby so I could concentrate to write. That would be the most wonderful gift you could ever give me."[10]

When Jesus calls people to discipleship, he doesn't motion in two directions—"Women and children to my left, you'll be judged on how well you followed someone else's calling; men, over here, you'll be judged on how well you followed your own calling." In the ministry and practice of Jesus you won't find him making special exceptions for women; he calls them to full discipleship.

In the next few chapters we will look at what the call of Jesus means: a call not only to follow but to gain self-recognition, to move beyond roles and find our callings. These are all part of following the voice of Jesus.

7
Unmasking
Our Identity

Six women and three men were in my writers' workshop class. We spent class periods and the weeks between reading books about writing and discussing what helps and hinders us as writers. During our fourth meeting, one older student named Teresa spoke up: "What I've realized is that it's impossible for me to sit down to write unless the house is completely tidy, beds are made and supper is cooking and there's bread rising. Oh, and maybe some cookies made."

Naomi, also a middle-aged woman, broke in. "The laundry done, not to mention the ironing. And no one else can want the computer. If my husband needs it or one of my daughters, then I have to wait."

"The thing is," said Teresa, "I really love to write. I've never enjoyed anything as much. When I write, I feel like I'm using my gifts, doing what God called me to do. I love it so much . . . that I somehow don't feel like I deserve to do it. It's only just hit me that's how I feel."

"I know exactly what you mean," Naomi said. "I feel like it's selfish because it's something I want to do. And I can't do something that I feel is self-indulgent."

In Ira Levin's book *The Stepford Wives* and the movie by the same name, perfect wives are formed as the women are made into automated puppets. But first, of course, the real person must be captured and killed.

In the same way, the transformation of a living, breathing individual woman into a domestic angel is no easy task. It involves, as we have seen, telling women that many things are Christian and biblical which are not.

But for a woman to buy this lie—the story of the domestic angel as a script for her life—involves several steps. The first and most important is that the woman must have her sense of who she is surgically removed. Otherwise, when someone gives her the message "Spending time to find out what you are called to do and doing it— why, that's self-indulgent!" she would laugh and say, "Of course it's not."

There are other steps in the creation of this domestic angel. As we will see in chapter eight, the woman will be asked to so fully clothe herself in different roles that she'll struggle to remember who she is. And by this point she may be paralyzed in terms of finding and following a call (chapter nine), which makes Satan very happy.

Under the Masks: Knowing Self

Women have been taught to be terrified of their own selfishness and self-indulgence. At a deep level most of us believe that to pay attention to who we are and how we feel is detrimental to that most important element of our lives—duty.

Christians often fear preoccupation with self, but for most Christian women I know, this is not a problem. Many have very little sense of themselves as created children of God, as authentic persons. Preoccupation with self is not a problem; acknowledging self is.

Jesus knew that self-knowledge was a crucial part of discipleship, and part of his call to men and women alike was (and is) the call to self-recognition. In fact, for a woman to find herself in relation to God, she needs a sense of who she is. How can I bring myself to God while I am wearing all these masks? How can I come to God when I am not sure who is underneath them? To grow as Christians we must grow in the love of God and grow in holiness. Both of these involve self-knowledge.

Perhaps Martha hoped, as she scurried around doing her duty, that she might once again suppress any self-knowledge. In essence, she says to Jesus, "I'm acting as the perfect woman. My sister is being horribly self-indulgent—look at her sitting there doing what she wants to do—listening to you. It shouldn't be allowed. Tell her to get up and help me do what women ought to do." Someone should have told Martha that a person who wanted to properly suppress any self-knowledge ought to carefully avoid asking Jesus.

Many women are so consumed with a sense of who they ought to be or so pressured by the demands of people around them that they are oblivious to their own feelings. They have lost the ability not only to speak about their feelings but also even to feel them. Listen to what these women say.

Nora, a social worker, stays at home caring for her two small children. "I'm thirty-five, and I've only just realized that I usually have no idea what I think and feel about things. Always in the past I've felt that it didn't really matter, because it didn't make any difference how I felt about stuff. My job was to get on and do what I needed to do, to do my duty. Feelings were a complicating factor. And if once I started to think about how I was feeling about something, who knows where it might end?"

Nancy is the head of her department at a university, a very strong, intelligent woman and a single mother of two daughters. But she admits that on the weekends when she doesn't have the children, she doesn't know what to do. "I've always been so busy with my work and my family," she says, "that I'm realizing that I don't even know what I like to do."

Mandy always seemed fine. She was a photographer and a mother of one young son. But this is what she told me: "I've just realized over the past two months that I'd completely switched off my feelings. Over a number of years I'd lost a sense that I could be happy, that I could know a life which was richer and fuller than the one I had. I guess I felt sort of disappointed with my marriage, motherhood, what my life was turning out like. If a crisis came up I would try to figure out how my mother, my husband, my boss or my son would feel about it. If I felt the glimmer of desire, of eagerness about something, I would bury it deeply because it seemed too painful to consider what those feelings might mean."

Lack of ability to explore one's feelings, fears of selfishness and self-indulgence: these are all part of the baggage the domestic angel brings when she moves in to take over our lives.

The self needs to be known.

The false self, created under command of the domestic angel, is the self that needs to die.

Jesus called people to self-recognition. When Nicodemus came to Jesus, he pushed him: Even you, a teacher of Israel—you need to start fresh (John 3:1-21). When Zacchaeus climbed the tree to see Jesus, Jesus was able to see a better self in Zacchaeus, and told him to scramble down and become that true self (Luke 19:2-8). Over and over again, Jesus pushed Peter to greater self-recognition.

The only people Jesus couldn't get through to were the Pharisees, so focused were they on the externals of life. Jesus pushed them toward self-recognition, and they refused the invitation. Jesus' parable of the two men coming into the temple in prayer is about knowing the self. The sinner, aware of his need, has brought himself to God, and he goes away justified. The other man can get nowhere because he's trying to get appearances right (Luke 18:9-14).

Under the Masks: Authentic Personhood

Jesus himself was the epitome of a person with a strong sense of authentic personhood, of who he was in relationship to God. This gave

Jesus the freedom to move among others in love and to fulfill his calling. Because of his strong sense of identity, Jesus knew when to say yes and when to say no.

To begin to follow Jesus, women need to get in touch with their identity and true personhood. This should seem obvious, but it isn't. Often Christian women have been taught exactly the opposite; they've been taught to suppress every sense of who they are and what they feel strongly about, to cement these under the hard surface of duty.

In fact, it's hard for Christians to even talk about this area. Authentic personhood is called a number of things in secular literature. Often when psychologists talk about this issue it is in terms of identity, of self, of authenticity, words that may not be helpful to us as Christians. Particularly the word *self* has negative connotations of selfishness, of something we ought to get rid of and crucify, rather than something we should find and acknowledge. We need to recognize the authentic person who God created to love and serve and follow Jesus.

When Jesus met the woman of Samaria near a well, he spoke to her (violating norms of the time) and offered her his living water. But it seems that before he could give her this living water, she needed to admit some things about who she was. "Go and fetch your husband," said Jesus. He knew that for this woman to grow spiritually, she needed to look at her life and make some changes.

Jesus pushed her toward self-recognition gently, but he didn't let her off the hook. The religious leaders in town ostracized and pointed fingers until she could only come to the well at a time of day when she would meet no one. Jesus confronted her and asked her to confront herself.

Jesus must have been able to look through the image this woman was projecting to see her real self. It was to this woman that Jesus revealed his true mission and calling, that he was the Messiah (John 4:26). She, in turn, became an evangelist to her whole city. This woman, sinful and fallen, but pushed to see herself and recognize Jesus, became the first evangelist to non-Jews. She followed. But first she had to recognize herself (John 4:1-42).

Masks Against Self-Recognition: Expert Opinion

Self and identity are often associated with selfishness in women's minds, perhaps because identity became a common theme through the work of psychologist Erik Erikson (who also coined the term *identity crisis*). Erikson believed that identity is formed through separation. As the toddler differentiates himself from his mother and the teen separates from his church and its values, so the person comes to a sense of identity, of self. Women have begun to question Erikson's paradigm of identity formation, as research has shown that women often come to a sense of who they are less by separation and more within a web of relationships.

Male experts have always had many opinions on the emotional status of women and the probable causes of their feelings of unhappiness and emptiness. Erikson helpfully suggested that the reason a woman is emotional during her menstrual periods is because she feels the traumatic loss of an opportunity to have a baby. He went on to say that this loss becomes the extraordinary pain of the emptiness in her life.[1] The esteemed Sigmund Freud told women that if they were feeling unhappy, the answer was to have another baby. For years other male experts have told women that menopause is a traumatic and awful time in their lives. In surveying women themselves—now there's an extraordinary idea—researchers have found that most women feel better during and after menopause than they did before. Men, believing that women's main use was her childbearing function, assumed that postmenopausal women were miserable and unproductive, but actually many women move into their most creative stage after menopause.[2]

Men are willing to give expert advice, and women are willing to take it. Articles in women's magazines offer helpful hints from men on attracting them, keeping them, making them happy in bed. (Notice how few articles there are by women giving advice to men in men's magazines.) Horoscopes, with advice from the stars, run almost exclusively in women's magazines.

Masks Against Self-Recognition: The Self from Outside

Women have been pushed away from self-recognition by expert advice; they also view themselves in a warped mirror, always from the perspective of someone on the outside.

Women have been trained to look at themselves, particularly their bodies, through the eyes of men. Advertisements and articles in women's magazines encourage women to see themselves as they might look to the male eye.

I was in a drugstore waiting in line. The cashier said to the woman in front of me, "I love your nails."

"I like yours too," the woman replied.

"Don't you think it odd that some women don't do their nails?" said the cashier.

"It's so important to a woman's presentation of herself," said the other woman. "Her nails are one of the first things about her that are seen, and they make such an impression."

I stood behind these two looking at my own nails. *Who's got time?* I thought. I can imagine that a person might do her nails for fun, just as some people dress up to go to the theater or out to dinner. But to consider one's presentation, as if one were always performing for an audience . . . But, I remembered, that's what women have been told to do. It's not what you're like inside, it's not who you are, it's not even what you do—it's how you present yourself, the impression you make.

High heels were never invented for a woman's ease in walking or so that she'd feel feminine. They were designed to make her buttocks stick out and make her unable to walk with ease. By comparison, men have barely tampered with their bodies.

Appearance, not accomplishments—that's what women have been taught to value in themselves. Depending on the time and place, this might mean they have their feet crippled by binding or wear whalebone stays and corsets (which sometimes exerted twenty to eighty pounds in pressure on a woman's body).[3]

From earliest childhood girls are taught to see themselves from the outside. The women that people our fairy tales are beautiful. (Well, the good ones are beautiful, and the bad ones are ugly.) Children's movies and toys encourage girls to focus on externals, giving underlying messages that the Barbie look is the one to strive for. Though no one's perfect—even Miss America contestants use tape to get their beautiful bodies just right—girls learn to evaluate themselves ruthlessly on the outside. Teen magazines focus on the exteriors of makeup and dress, and they print photos of women's fashion bloopers.

Masks Against Self-Recognition: The Romance Script
Why should women be so concerned to present themselves as beautiful? Because we all believe that beautiful women get what they want. An ugly man (we'd call him "cute") may marry a beautiful woman, but if an ugly woman marries a good-looking man we are shocked (unless perhaps she's very, very wealthy and preferably very, very old). Old women—who have little beauty—are less valuable in our culture. They are often looked down on, while old men are considered distinguished or eccentric.

If a younger woman marries an older man, we are not shocked (even though women live longer than men). If the reverse happens, we feel that something is wrong. Why? Because it is beautiful women who get what they want.

We believe these myths about women because we have heard them a million times in fairy tales, cartoons, sitcoms, soaps, movies, novels.

Deep in our heart of hearts we believe that a good woman will be found by a man and married. It is the story that ends, "And they lived happily ever after." The story of a woman's life has been handed to her as one of romance that ends in marriage. The wedding day is the high point of her life. Yeah, well, there might be kids, but it's really all downhill from the wedding day.

This makes life rough for the unmarried, of course. No matter how stimulating her calling, her ministry, the single woman feels unwhole somehow, as if she's been robbed of the most important part of life.

But it's also disastrous for the married who see their lives primarily in terms of this romance, rather than in terms of their primary relationship with Jesus.

Boys see themselves in quests and adventures; these are the stories that they are told. Sometimes there is a beautiful princess involved, but she's really a reward or a benefit. The real deal is the quest, the adventure, the lifelong search for something, whether it be a grail or fame or self-understanding.

These stories get under our skin. We believe them at such a deep level that we forget to compare them with the One True Story that is found in the Gospels. In that story men and women alike are involved in a great quest, a wonderful adventure.

I spoke about these two different life scripts—the romance and the quest—to a group of college students. A young man came up to me afterward. "That's the problem with a Christian college—what you said about the romance and quest stories."

"Tell me more," I said.

"Well, the young women come to college with no idea of a life, of things they want to do, of places they want to go, of career aspirations. From the Christian homes they've been raised in, the churches they've attended and the stories they've read, they come with this romance story in their minds. They are here to fulfill their main goal—to meet Prince Charming and get married.

"The young men arrive with a strong sense of a life ahead of them—a life in which they will need to earn money, provide for a family, have a career, perhaps be involved in a ministry. They are here, really, to prepare for the quest before them."

"So tell me why you see this as a problem."

"Women are always complaining about the guys. They say they never date. Guys are scared to date because they sense the power of the romance script in the women they meet. And meanwhile they've got to get on with their quest."

We should be shocked that so many Christian students are not seeking God's call, but a white knight who will bring them happiness.

What if these women—who have so totally bought the domestic angel line that their only concern is about their need to find a partner—brought similar enthusiasm to knowing God's call?

The power of the romance and quest scripts even worm their way into Christian college students' use of the Bible, according to a recent study. Seniors do use the Bible and prayer to seek God's guidance: he wants to know God's plan for his career; she wants to know God's plan in terms of finding Mr. Right.[4] They've traded in the true biblical model, which would call both to discipleship and a life of following Christ, for a story told to them, over and over, by the "world."

Masks Against Self-Recognition: Deception

Encouraged to see themselves from the outside, encouraged to believe in a white knight who will come and carry them off and give them happiness, many women do what comes naturally—they improve the packaging and pay little attention to what really counts.

Women have been told that it's okay to use feminine wiles to make themselves attractive to men. Although it is deceptive, acting passive and helpless has been a way for women to be successfully feminine, to protect or bolster others.[5] They have learned an important lesson: "The weaker sex must protect the stronger sex from recognizing the strength of the weaker sex lest the stronger sex feel weakened by the strength of the weaker sex."[6]

And women have been encouraged to be deceptive to each other; after all, they are locked in mortal combat for the all-important male. These competitive games steal from women the language to talk about their lives. I once spent an evening with a group of women who had been living in a dorm together for three years. I asked them to talk with each other about the pressures they felt about appearance and getting a diamond before they left college. After they talked at great length, several confided in me that in their three years together, they had never discussed these issues. When I asked why, they told me. Competition.

Women are encouraged to use their clothes and bodies to deceive.

We do it so naturally that it seems completely normal to us "to lie with our bodies: to bleach, redden, unkink or curl our hair, pluck eyebrows, shave armpits, wear padding in various places or lace ourselves, take little steps, glaze finger and toenails, wear clothes that emphasized our helplessness."[7]

These deceptions with our bodies, with men, with other women lead to deceptions within ourselves. We put ourselves into a deep sleep, losing the real person at the heart of ourselves.

So Carefully Masked: The Real Fear

Why are we willing to don these masks, to hide from knowledge of ourselves? Why was Martha willing to frantically peel onions when the Lord of Life was sitting in her living room? I believe that behind our willingness to wear masks lies the most fundamental of all our fears: the fear of being truly known.

We believe that if we were truly known we would not be loved. Many of us in our heart of hearts believe this: if that close friend could really see into my soul, she would see me for who I really am and no longer like me. We believe that to be known means not to be loved. We believe this about other people, and we believe it about God.

Kerry had always been a wonderful student, first in her high-school class in Seattle, later graduating with honors from her college in Oregon. She went to graduate school in Tennessee, studying linguistics for several years. At the end of the program she had to take major exams. She flunked them.

Kerry had never flunked a test in her life. To flunk her M.A. exam was devastating. She took months to recover. Her whole sense of herself was wrapped up in her academic achievement. Her sense of who she was included the good student, the smart person. Her plans for the future required her academic success.

Twenty years later, Kerry counts this experience as the most important in her life. She learned that academic success was not as important as many other things. She was forced to rethink her life goals, and she realized that she wanted to go forward in another field. But most of all, she says, she realized that there is grace.

Kerry explained to me that she realized that God's love for her was not based on her performance. God loved her as Kerry. And God had much grace to give her as she lived her life. Kerry was liberated. She could put the burden of her life at the feet of Jesus and trust him, knowing she was loved.

Kerry became aware, through her traumatic failure, that she hadn't really trusted in a loving God. She believed that she had to perform to be loved. This fear of not being loved by God underlies all our fears and pushes us to mask ourselves and race distractedly and frantically through our lives. This is the really big fear: that God doesn't love me.

The Biggest of All Masks: Trying to Earn God's Love

Sometimes I ask audiences to write brief endings to these three statements:

1. God loves me because . . .
2. God loves me, therefore . . .
3. God would love me more if . . .

Take a few minutes and fill in the blanks yourself. Then put the piece of paper away somewhere.

To be able to lower ourselves to our knees, to sit at the feet of Jesus, we must have at some deep level a belief that we are loved by God. Even if we believe (theologically) that God loves us unconditionally, we easily slip into believing that we have to earn God's love.

Why don't we believe that God loves us?

Our inability to believe in God's love stems from many sources. Perhaps our sense of alienation goes back to the original Fall in the Garden of Eden. And the enemy is always quick to assure us that we are not loved or lovable.

For many people, their inability to believe they are loved is related to the way they were raised, perhaps by parents who taught them that they were more worthy of love if they performed in certain ways. Those who carry memories of demeaning and distant fathers or demanding mothers often carry these over to their ideas of God.

Sometimes religion has projected a false god, an Oz-like wizard, so that followers can be more easily manipulated. Focusing on external rules that please God (as did their brother Pharisees before them), these fundamentalists incur fear. A God who loves unconditionally is useless, but a God who loves you better if you behave is of infinite value to someone who wants to manipulate others. But the preachers are not solely to blame. People in the pews often prefer heavy-handed, small-minded religion because it's simpler.

Parental influence and religious manipulation can twist into a strong rope. Historian Doug Frank has studied the backgrounds of the great men of evangelicalism and found that many of them had absent or very threatening fathers. He argues that they transferred this to their relationships with God, at a time when American evangelicalism was being formed. The result: many evangelicals have learned a God who is modeled on the manipulative, neglectful fathers of these men.[8]

Many Christians, for all these reasons, believe that if they were better, God would love them more. Christians find some of this God's demands difficult but possible to fulfill. "If I brought more people to Christ," or "if I studied his Word, the Holy Bible, more," or "if my lifestyle were more Christian and righteous," or "if I talked to him more often," or "if I didn't sin as much"—these are some of the qualities people list when I ask them what would make them feel more presentable to God.

But some demands are so vague that no one could ever fulfill them. What is the magic key to winning the love of this God? Could it be, as individuals suggest, that God would love me more if

☐ I believed in him more.

☐ I could not be swayed.

☐ I followed him more.

☐ I was obedient to him twenty-four hours a day.

☐ I would follow his Word and teachings.

☐ I tried to be a stronger person in Christ.

☐ I listened to his voice.

☐ I would totally sell out for him.

☐ I would let go and let God.

☐ I praised and thanked him enough.

☐ I was more Christian.

☐ I learned to love more.

☐ I didn't take him for granted.

These Christians desperately want God's love, but they've been told that to receive it they need to get better, lay everything on the altar, have their quiet time more regularly—it's up to them.[9]

Yes, I believe that God would like to love me, if only I could make myself good enough for God. There are a number of ways I could do that. Most are impossible, of course, or at least impossible to do all the time or well enough. So I guess I can never know I'm truly loved, or at least loved enough to wallow in God's love or allow my life to flow out of that love.

So what is the answer? Maybe as long as I don't look within, I won't see my flaws and God won't notice them either.

Look at your answers to the questions about God's love. Do you really believe that God loves you, just as you are?

For the answers we give to these questions are really answers to a different question: What is God like?

Often we have been encouraged to believe in a God who is "a false and uncaring God, who binds at exactly the point where the true God sets free and who wounds at exactly the point where the true God heals."[10] This is the God created, according to Doug Frank, by the (all-male, of course) evangelicals early in the twentieth century, in the image of the heavy-handed but absent American father.

We pull our masks very firmly in place for this frightening God who is only very distantly related to Jesus Christ, because we are desperately afraid to look within, to bring ourselves to God.

Jesus' Call
People can be made good (at least for a while) through manipulation

and fear. They will desperately, madly perform to a certain standard. (And there's a biblical precedent for this: the Pharisees lived their lives this way.)

Or people can be made good by association. The one who feels loved and sits at the feet of Jesus will be good because she loves and is loved. She will seek greater self-knowledge because she knows that is how she will be made more Christlike. She will spend time in the Scriptures to get to know her lover better. And she will be able to seek more self-knowledge because she knows she is loved. Unconditionally loved.

Near the top of the New Testament's list of most courageous people is the sinful woman who anoints Jesus at Simon the Pharisee's home (Luke 7:36-50). Picture the scene.

The guests, selected from the religious establishment, sit, arms crossed, deeply convinced of their moral superiority. Jesus is a guest. I can almost hear the conversation at the table: "Let's see what this controversial rabbi has to say, shall we?"

Then the pendulum swings from comfortable respectability to shocked disgust. Almost as if someone started pulling off their clothes in church, here, in a Pharisee's home, is a filthy woman, a prostitute. She weeps, anoints Jesus' feet, kisses them and uses her hair to dry them. Poor Simon. By now, of course, Jesus has been made unclean. The rest of the room may also be unclean—Simon will need to consult the rule book and see. And everyone's lost their appetite. Poor Simon. His own home, and here are his friends, and he puts them into this dreadfully embarrassing situation. For a respectable religious leader, for a host—my goodness, what an uncomfortable situation!

For everyone but Jesus. Jesus is the only one who cares less about respectability than he does about truth.

What made it possible for this woman to confront the hostile stares, the despising glances of these men? Somehow, somewhere she must have encountered the love of Jesus.

The room is filled with the aroma of the perfume, the embarrass-ment of the respectable, the love of Jesus and the adoration of this sinful woman. All the options are here: self-recognition and a decision to follow Jesus on the one hand; self-satisfied unwillingness to confront the self on the other. Jesus pronounces this sinful woman forgiven, known and loved: she can walk straight into the kingdom, head held high. Simon? He'll be left pounding on the door. He doesn't get it. But she has looked within, seen her need and allowed Jesus to touch her.

8
Stepping out
of Roles &
off the Pedestal

*B*efore you begin reading this chapter, take a few minutes to write down five or six answers to the question, Who am I?

Working Against Self-Recognition: Roles
It has taken me almost twenty years to figure out why I dislike being a minister's wife. It has little to do with my husband's busy work schedule, disastrously frantic Easters and Christmases, anonymous letters or even calls at odd hours of the day and night. Those don't really bother me. What I dislike are the expectations that I be a certain way, or at least play a particular role.

People's expectations of a minister's wife vary from culture to culture and from denomination to denomination. At present I feel fortunate to be in a place and denomination that allow me freedom as a minister's wife. Other women aren't so blessed. I've talked to many ministers' wives about the pressures they feel, pressures to dress in a particular way—nothing too shabby, but nothing so nice that it might imply unseemly luxury—pressures to head the women's group, teach Sunday school, cook pretty well and even play the piano. Some ministers' wives seem to like performing this role. But I have yet to meet one who under the surface feels really comfortable and able to be herself. I would love to meet one.

What feels suffocating—almost claustrophobic—about being a minister's wife is the feeling you get from some people that it's not you they want. They don't want to see beyond the mask of "the minister's wife," which bears an uncanny resemblance to the domestic angel. They want you to play a certain part, not to be yourself, not to have a life as a human being, but just to be a minister's wife, kind of like first-graders who assume that their teachers sleep at school because they exist only as teachers. Perhaps they find some comfort in thinking that there is a domestic angel out there, a supermother perhaps, who never loses her cool, always has time to get the children to church (preferably for several services) looking like their clothes fit them and have been washed (and maybe even ironed!), who always smiles and is polite and ever so good. (Does she become that way through endless close association with her holy husband?)

But this puts the minister's wife in an awkward position. Perhaps she plays the game: she allows herself to be placed on a pedestal where people can look up to her with admiration, people like the member of our church in Cape Town who said to me as we dried teacups, "Mrs. Ashcroft, you have a very godly bearing."

A pedestal is a very uncomfortable place. Think about it. There you are, unable to move more than a foot in any direction with all these people looking at you, admiration shining in their faces. You can stand there for quite a while, but it begins to feel awful. You are aware that there are other parts of you that the admiring group can't see.

I stand there on the pedestal, thinking, *Okay, how does my bearing look now—godly enough, or has it slipped a bit?*

But when the pedestal feels too restricting, you have few options. Perhaps rebellion? Many ministers' wives get to the point where they would do almost anything to get off the pedestal.

So I could have suddenly cracked and made faces at my admirers and said, "A godly bearing—you think so, huh?!"

No wonder so many ministers' wives get sick, depressed, suicidal: they are put into a dreadful position. They are asked to keep up appearances, to act a part. They have an impossible job description— to keep everyone happy—and none of the power with which to do it.

Working Against Self-Recognition: The Pedestal
As we have seen, the "domestic angel" is best when she is exalted, out of reach, looked up to and admired.

In South Africa it seemed to me that minister's wives were very good. A good minister's wife would not have her own job or her own ministry, but she should definitely be at every service, conference and meeting, and make countless cups of tea.

The church rectory was directly across the street from Christ Church. My husband's office was in the house, so our living room functioned as a sort of doctor's waiting room. I plied people who were waiting for him with cups of tea and homemade cookies, and of course apologized for him if he was running late. (My son learned to play all this to his advantage, moving from one waiting person to the next, getting them to read books to him. I'd take in the next round of tea, and he'd be sitting on the lap of a nun. Once he was sitting next to a recovering alcoholic who was dragging on a cigarette between pages of the book.)

On Sunday mornings the living room and porch were used for a nursery, and sometimes fifty or sixty kids and the nursery workers would come into the house. One Sunday morning about forty-five minutes before the main service started I was sitting in the living room with my two-and-a-half-year-old, Andrew. I was very pregnant and hadn't slept well the night before; my varicose veins were hurting a lot. I gave Andrew a cup of milky tea. He spilled it on the carpet. I poured him another cup and told him to be careful. He squealed with glee and turned it upside down, pouring it down the front of his church clothes and all over the couch. I lost my temper.

I don't swear as a general rule, but I snatched him and the cup up and stomped into our kitchen. "Damn the tea, damn the couch, damn, damn, damn!" My mutter rose to a shout. I opened the kitchen door as I roared the last "damn," and there was a young couple I'd never met standing in the kitchen.

I looked at them and tried to think what to say.

"I don't believe we've ever met" didn't quite seem appropriate.

"Welcome to Christ Church House" seemed wrong somehow.

So did "So nice to meet you. I was hoping you'd pop in."

I mumbled something about Andrew spilling his tea again, and they just looked at me. I paused, expecting that they might explain their presence.

"This is our first time visiting Christ Church," said the young man. "My wife got something in her throat and needed a drink of water, and the usher sent us over here to get some."

After that meeting I'd occasionally be at a church gathering and someone would bring this young couple over to me and say, "Dan and Francis, have you met Mary Ellen?"

"Yes, we've met," they'd say.

I liked being around Dan and Francis. I always felt liberated around them because they knew I wasn't a wonderfully nice minister's wife. I didn't feel they expected me to be something I wasn't.

My first official task as minister's wife at St. Stephen's Church in Minnesota was to speak at a women's meeting. The first thing I told them was about my experience with Dan and Francis. I told them this story hoping that people wouldn't admire me, that they wouldn't pedestal me. But we shouldn't have to swear to get off our pedestal.

There are many other roles besides that of minister's wife. How about the role of missionary's wife? (Odd that there's no role of missionary's husband.) There's the doctor's wife, the politician's wife. Or somebody's wife, somebody's mom, somebody's daughter.

Roles are great in the theater. And at times we have to play them in the rest of life. But when we spend too much time playing different roles, it can rob us of our sense of the person at the center of the roles. Instead of the integrated self, we find ourselves disintegrated. Soon we can't find that person at all.

While this pressure to appear a certain way is especially strong on ministers' wives, I think all women feel it. The pressure to present a front of ever-smiling sweetness and keep the raging resentments and emotions carefully stuffed underneath can be terrible for women. In psychologist Lisa Sinclair's study "The Role of Unresolved Anger in the Psychosocial Dysfunction of Missionary Wives," she finds that missionary wives are often debilitated and their useful ministries crippled by the loneliness and pressures of the role.[1]

Constant role-playing is disastrous. It works against women's good mental health, pushing them toward anxiety and depression. It works against women's sense of self-knowledge, leading them to focus on the externals rather than the internals. And it runs absolutely counter to the call of Jesus. Jesus called people to a consistency between the outer and inner person.

Externals, like the religious practice of the Pharisees and the role-playing of the sweet minister's wife, have a way of deadening us to our true selves. Jesus' ministry was a wake-up call. *Repent* means pay attention, look alive!

The High Cost of Coping

Jesus' call to Martha was a call to stop playing a role and climb off the pedestal. She could have gone on for years, just keeping her head above water in a domestic frenzy. Jesus saw beyond her activities and told her to stop coping.

We might expect women to be in a better position than men to respond to the call of Jesus. Women's vulnerability, weakness and helplessness can be one of their greatest strengths, according to psychologist Jean Baker Miller. Their recognition of their need can become for women a key to life and growth.[2] But it's difficult. It is easier for a woman to remain in the roles than to step out of them.[3]

Why would women cheerfully accept roles? Because they provide a way to cope. In fact, one of the biggest problems many women face is their excellent coping skills.

There's the student who has been involved for six months in an abusive relationship. The man beats her up and tries to talk her into sex. She wants to break up with him, but she thinks it might affect his relationship with the Lord and then she would be responsible. She feels terrible, but she can cope.

There's Hannah, who drives her daughter and her boyfriend to a basketball game. They make out as she chauffeurs them. She feels furious but can't speak to them. She masters her anger and goes back to coping.

There's Nancy, who has a job she hates doing work she despises. Everyone appreciates her smiling face and her efficiency. Especially the boss, it turns out, and he tells her how much he appreciates her, and how he really thinks the world of her and if only his wife were as nice to him as she is. Nancy swallows her revulsion and copes.

A woman may continue to cope through crises of many different kinds—physical, emotional and sexual abuse, illness, disability, sudden death of a spouse, betrayal by a loved one, financial pressures, loss of a job, a move, a parental divorce. With each successive crisis she may be filled with anxiety and stress, but she copes.[4] She believes that she is doing the right thing. The Christian thing.

Unlike Jesus' call to women, the call many Christian women find compelling—to perform their duty and keep coping—is a call to oblivion. It demands that they shut down their emotions, that they deaden themselves to what gives them life, to their own souls, to their callings and their possibilities.

This is tragedy. A sweet smile is pasted over the pain; a silvery voice drowns the cry within. She is my neighbor and my friend, my fellow church member, this sweetly smiling woman. Her carefully taped-on smile reminds me of something. Where have I seen it before?

I know. It's the smile of the politician's wife. You know the picture:

he's admitting that he's had four affairs, and his wife is standing next to him, perfectly dressed, perfectly coifed, smiling just enough to show that she's supportive, but not delighted. And I wonder, *What is going on in that woman? Why doesn't she stick out her tongue at the photographer and then at her husband?* Because she has lost herself.

She's coping. But she's lost her authentic self where she might learn to be honest, integrated and strong. Possessed by the expectations of husband, children, church, husband's job, she feels pushed here and there by people's expectations. She's lost the ability to say no, to speak up for what she really believes. Years of the smile and the well-worn roles, and she finds that her inner self has gone to sleep.

Look closely at this woman. She depends on the Miss America tape; it holds her mouth in the perfect smile, while the truth of her despair and rage lurk beneath. Under the smile, under the roles, under the coping skills—a tiny spark of her (all that's left of her that even knows how to feel what she feels) knows that her life is slipping away. It's all slipping away, and she will be left with nothing.

Oh, everyone eventually goes to the grave with nothing. But she will have done none of the things she dreamed of as a girl. The hospital, the classroom, the lab . . . all are slipping away. She is losing the respect of her children, who are beginning to smirk at her for treating them like her masters. Her husband seems distant. And her eyes are the eyes of someone who is lost, someone who has—under a thousand demands, a thousand splintered roles—misplaced herself. She cannot look within. To keep coping, she cannot acknowledge the sparks of desire, rage and longing. To even for one second peek around the domestic angel's demands would be like opening Pandora's box. So she smiles and glides silently into oblivion.

Oh yes, a woman can cope. If she packs her feelings down a little harder, does what duty demands and says no to self, she can keep going for years. But does she want to live her life coping, getting it right on the surface while her soul suffers? Or does she want to thrive?

To thrive, a woman needs to be in touch with herself. She needs to respond to Jesus' call to focus on her soul and what will nourish it.

Instead of pulling her roles more tightly around her, she needs to step boldly off the pedestal.

The Push out of the Boat

We find endless ways to protect ourselves from the grace of God. There's a part of each of us that would prefer our own coping skills to God's radical healing touch. The Pharisees did it with their religious practice and their rules, and we do it by surrounding ourselves with comforts or being busy and respectable, playing our roles well. Our comforts, our roles, our rules—these become the walls we build around our hearts, around our very selves.

"My gosh, I have just heard that you have multiple sclerosis," I said to a woman in our church. "That must be very traumatic."

"Well, it was, but it's been a gift. An incredible gift."

"A gift?"

"Yes. I was a successful broker. My business had taken off, and I was running frantically all the time. Never took time to think about relationships, about God. I could have kept that up for years. With MS you can't do that. I've slowed down and discovered extraordinary things about myself, about life, about God. I can honestly say I'm thankful for it."

Who hasn't heard this story? A person is pushed past coping, and that push turns out to be the hand of God. What appears to be a lightning bolt of disaster turns out to be a gift of life in the hands of God. The terrible pain of a parting, a traumatic revelation about parents—anything can be transformed by God's gracious hands into the most wonderful blessing of our lives.

When we decide to stop coping or are moved beyond it by circumstances beyond our control, we allow God to strip away our armor. For some it may be a painful move or children going to college. It may be illness or divorce. (Studies show that women are often pushed toward greater identity growth through a crisis in their relational lives, unlike men, who are pushed toward greater identity through a career crisis.[5])

Coming to the end of ourselves, running out of coping skills, can seem like death. We've learned to keep up a brave front, for we fear loss of control and at all costs attempt to avoid a breakdown. As Pastor David Adams says,

Breakdown is talked about in hushed tones, as if it were a deadly sin. There are countless people avoiding breakdown by tranquilizing themselves one way or another. Breakdown often occurs when an old way of life or a relationship dies and we refuse to face it. We pour energies and resources to discover the "good old days" and we are not at ease in the present. . . . Breakdown is not the end. It is only part of the process of this earth. Without the cross there is no resurrection; without death, no newness of life. Without breakdown there is no breakthrough.[6]

God's grace often comes to us when we're forced to encounter our lives in a new way. When the rug of comfort and security is pulled out from under our feet, we find ourselves forced to trust and follow Jesus in a new way.

Zacchaeus and the rich young man both had money problems—they had too much money. But tax collector Zacchaeus had reached the end of his rope. The rich young man was perhaps a bit too wealthy, a bit too popular, a bit too young: he was nowhere near the end of his rope, and he couldn't let go and follow Jesus. Zacchaeus's loneliness, his sense of guilt, his shame—all these may have pushed him to despair. When the call of Jesus came, he was ready for it. He let go of the rope (as he scrambled down the tree) and started a new life.

Edith was the perfect suburban mother. She lived in her elegant luxury home in one of Atlanta's nicest suburbs. She had beautiful clothes, was a member of several fine clubs, had five healthy daughters. She played tennis and bridge and did some volunteer work at the children's school.

When her husband ran off with a stunning younger woman, her world seemed to come to an end. She had no skills; she felt she could hardly cope with her children. The house was sold, the memberships in the clubs dropped. It seemed there was nothing worth living for.

Edith talked to some wise people, got some career counseling and realized that she'd had a dream, ages ago. In fact it took her several months to remember her interest as a teen in helping teens who were pregnant.

Remembering the dream gave her the fire to take a huge risk. She returned to school and finished an educational psychology degree. Ten years later she has started several programs in schools for teens who are pregnant or who are parents. She is a radiant person and seems more fully alive than almost anyone I've met. I can't imagine what she was like before she took the extraordinary risk, before she decided to grow and to find out what God had gifted her for, what Christ was calling her to.

X-ed or Named

From the time of the earliest church, when people were baptized they were named. In Madeleine L'Engle book *A Wrinkle in Time,* naming is another word for loving, as a person is identified as who she is and called by name.

Because Jesus loves Martha, he calls her by name. She, the role-wrapped domestic angel who copes with any household crisis, comes to Jesus, and he speaks: "Martha, Martha." She might have preferred her roles to this naming. Being named, she is called to stop her coping, to take a risk and follow.

Jesus names all of us. "Mary Ellen," he says to me. He doesn't say, "Hey, you over there, Ernie's wife!" Or "Andrew, Stephen and Susannah's mom." Or "Mind if I just call you 'minister's wife'?"

The call of Jesus is to say yes to him above all else. The potential disciples who come with excuses of domestic chores and family relationships that they should put first, Jesus tells to fish or cut bait: stop making excuses and follow. "No one who puts a hand to the plow and looks back is fit for the kingdom of God" (Luke 9:62).

Often I would rather hide, cope or busy myself with frantic activities than be named. My roles as minister's helpmeet, wife, mother, teacher, writer can easily form a thick armor that keeps me from facing myself, from the tough work of growing in a life of discipleship.

Look at the answers you wrote at the beginning of this chapter. What did you say about yourself? How much of what you wrote was about doing, rather than being, about roles rather than yourself as deeply called and loved of God? No role, no skill in coping, no pedestal can protect us forever. The only firm foundation on which to build a life is one in which I know myself and bring that self to Jesus.

Ultimately we lose not only our houses and our possessions. We lose our friends and our families. All that we are left with is the authentic self, loved by Christ and called by him. The call of Jesus is to consistency, to integration; it is a call to find the self at the center of the roles.

9
Finding Our God-Given Calling

*B*efore you begin this chapter, stop for a moment and list four or five people—teachers, ministers, counselors or friends—who have had a major impact on your life, without whom you would be a very different person.

I think of Mrs. Holzer. In my high school, funding was limited, so classes were large and I had three study halls a day. School was infinitely boring to my seventeen-year-old mind. In fact, I hated school, and my greatest joy was to skip out and go walking on the beach, hanging out with my friends.

Somehow in my senior year I was put in Mrs. Holzer's honors English class. She gave us our reading list, and I nearly passed out. *The Iliad* and *The Odyssey* by Homer. *The Aeneid* by Virgil. Dante's *Inferno*. *Faust*. I was stunned. She expected us to read this stuff? An older woman with graying, curly hair and a spreading figure, she would walk into class with a stack of books and turn to us, and her face would light up. Within a week I was ecstatic about classical literature, wild about Dante. All I wanted to do was read. I asked her for other book suggestions. By the end of the semester, I knew that I wanted to read and write as much as possible. Maybe I would go to college after all.

I think of Ca Wood. When I was expecting our first son in Cape Town, South Africa, I felt like I was entering into totally new territory. I'd hardly been around babies, didn't really like them that much and felt overwhelmed by the prospect of having one. Ca, who had raised four delightful boys, took me under her wing. When I was exhausted by mothering, she would take Andrew and play with him. When I was very pregnant with Stephen and Andrew was two, I stayed with Ca and her husband while Ernie was away on a long trip. She showed me some of her favorite games that she played with children. She showed me how to make a picnic tea to break up a long afternoon. I came to see mothering as a wonderful calling.

I think of the counselor I saw when I was pushed past coping by a traumatic move. She knew how to ask the right, often probing and difficult questions so that I would take some new risks in my life. Without her wise pushing and challenging demands, I might have been stuck.

The list could go on and on.

Look at your list again as I look at mine.

What would your life be like if one or all of these people had not said yes to God? What if any of these people, gifted as they are, had declined God's calling on their lives? Where would you be?

Perhaps other people would have come along. But when I look at how these people have truly graced my life, challenging me to further growth, by following God's calling on their lives, I feel humbled. I am deeply indebted to these people who said yes to God's call.

God's Call

God calls people. Presumably God could do everything on his own—

pouf!—and that would be that. Instead God chooses to collaborate. He gifts people and calls them to use their talents in the service of others.

If we believe in a God who creates people and does indeed "have a wonderful plan for their lives," we will pursue that calling in our Christian journey. "Everyone has his own specific vocation or mission in life," says Stephen Covey in his popular book *The Seven Habits of Highly Effective People.* "Therein he cannot be replaced, nor can his life be repeated. Thus everyone's task is as unique as is his specific opportunity to implement it."[1]

In one sense every Christian's calling is the same: we are to follow Jesus Christ and to glorify him, to grow in holiness and godliness, to bring others to him, to use our gifts for Christ. But our callings are also different, because God in his wisdom decided to use humans to work in the world. For Christians, our callings are part of the wonderful tapestry of God's work. We do what we are called to do, and God weaves our lives in with the lives of others, making a wonderful work of art.

For as long as I can remember I have loved words, reading and writing. When I was a toddler I invented my own language, which seemed to me to fit with reality better than English. (My one problem was that no one else seemed to understand it!) Through junior high, I read all the time, wrote elaborate poems and stories. As an undergraduate I studied literature and writing. I worked for some years in a library, telling stories and encouraging people to read. When my children were small, I read to them for hours, wrote letters home from the mission field and read through most of Western literature. I went back to school and finished a degree in English and went on to get a Ph.D. in English. Now I teach literature and writing. And I write.

My love of reading and writing is an essential part of who I am. My calling, therefore, is part of my identity, part of the person God created me to be. That "created personhood" is complex. It includes what I enjoy, my personality traits, my abilities to be close to a certain number of people, my Myers-Briggs type, my lack of ability to remember details, my love of nature, and so on. Many of these things I know about myself now were nascent in my childhood. At times in my life my paid work has overlapped with my calling, and at other times it hasn't. Always, though, my calling is a part of who I am.

"If the whole body were an eye," Paul asks in the book of Corinthians (1 Corinthians 12:12-31), "where would the hearing be? If the whole body were hearing, where would the sense of smell be?" Our minds conjure up a grotesque picture of a giant eye sitting in a chair or a huge ear walking down the hall, and that's what Paul intended. He wanted the Christians at Corinth to see that it was ridiculous for the church to expect people to have the same gifts and callings.

The church has done a pretty good job of expecting men to have a variety of gifts and callings—as long as those don't include childcare, nurturing responsibilities or anything to do with making coffee or food preparation. But the church has often limited what women can do to extend the kingdom.

What could be more painful than when God calls a woman and the church slams a door in her face, because God's call must take back seat to the precepts of men? Often women who have had a clear sense of calling from God to a teaching and preaching ministry had no option but to go overseas as missionaries, because denominations taught that it was okay for women to be active in a teaching/preaching role as long as their recipients were children or natives. (There are some churches even today that suggest that women can teach males up to a certain age, and then their exercise of their God-given gifts would be damaging to postpubic male minds!)

In stark contrast with this is the teaching of the New Testament.

Jesus called women to follow him as disciples. The earliest church assumed women's ministries based on gifts and callings, not on gender. Women prophesied, they taught, they prayed, they served. One was an apostle.[2]

God's Design

Calling assumes God's creative genius. It also assumes that God wants to use humans on the basis of their gifts and callings, as he did in the early church. God has given the gifts; he has set the calling on our hearts. Our part is to pay attention and actively pursue the calling.

When my father had major heart surgery, my mother and I stayed for five days in Providence Hospital in Seattle. This was the most I'd ever been around hospitals, nurses, doctors, patients. Ever since my idea that maybe I'd be a nurse was shattered when I sewed the stuffing into a Thanksgiving turkey at age nine (and it gave me the creeps), I'd avoided medical stuff.

But as I talked to my dad's surgeon, I found that he obviously loved the challenge of heart surgery. I talked to the intensive care nurses, and they clearly liked what they did.

Spending days, weeks, years in a hospital would be hell to me. Perhaps for the intensive care nurse, the idea of being in a classroom or sitting at a computer working with words would be hell. God has made us different, giving us different gifts, ministries and callings. At Providence I felt so grateful that I hadn't been called to medical work. I had to remind myself that in keeping with the name of the hospital, if I'd been called I probably would have loved it. I kept thanking God that there were others who were called to do medical work.

I suspect there are mornings when the nurses and doctors at Providence Hospital don't want to get up and go to work. But in general, when people follow God's plan and pursue their callings, they find joy in their souls, and good is done for others.

I believe that God designed people to feel fully alive when they are pursuing their callings. This urge to be creative and active, Dorothy L. Sayers argues, is the image of God on humankind. In the book of Genesis, when we are told that humanity is created in God's image, all we know of God is that God creates. God made this, God made that. "Not presumably because He had to, but because He wanted to. He made light and water, and earth and birds and fish and animals and enjoyed what He had done. And then He 'made man in his own image'—a creature in the image of a Creator."[3]

This is the stamp of God on human life—that people thrive on challenge and creativity. This has been confirmed by University of Chicago psychologist Mihaly Csikszentmihalyi. He started studying what makes people happy, asking them to talk or write about experiences in which they had felt the most joy. Then he looked at these narratives for consistency. What he found surprised him. People were happiest when they felt most challenged. When they were pulled out of themselves, working on something that really grabbed them—that was when people experienced the greatest satisfaction. Csikszentmihalyi went on to study a wide variety of people, living all over the world, working in widely varied jobs, functioning with different levels of education. The word most often used by this diverse group to characterize their happiness was *flow*. (Csikszentmihalyi's book goes by that one-word title.)

Csikszentmihalyi was surprised that people experienced moments of tremendous happiness even in times of great deprivation, such as in concentration camps or during the London blitz. External circumstances had little to do with happiness or "flow." What seemed to matter most was the sense of being caught up in something challenging and demanding, a calling, a "dedication to a cause greater than oneself."[4] A person is happiest when her mind or body is "stretched to its limits by voluntary action to accomplish something difficult and worthwhile," giving her a sense of mastery and participation in life.[5] A person's leisure time was often least fulfilling, unless she was doing something challenging like painting or mountain climbing, because time spent passively often left people feeling empty, dull and dissatisfied.[6] The person who experiences flow least is the one distracted and scattered by small demands, as was Martha.

People will be happiest when they are pursuing a God-given, challenging calling. The call of Jesus to women is the call to active ministry, but the calling to be a domestic angel often robs them of meaning and challenge.

Finding Our Calling: Looking Back
Calling springs from God's creation. Our identities are a woven pat-

tern of what we do well, what we care deeply about, what we enjoy, where we like to be. Clearly life circumstances build on these propensities. Who knows? Perhaps my children, who were all born in Africa, will have deep within them a love for that continent that will draw them back someday.

Life circumstances can bury our callings. Girls, especially, tend to lose a sense of themselves as gifted when their self-esteem plummets from the age of ten onward. Many girls lose the ability to express what they know, believe and want.[7]

Career counselors try to help women remember. They ask them to list eight to ten experiences they had before the age of twelve in which they felt great about what they did. After listing these, they are asked to choose four that stand out and write about them in some detail. Then with the help of the counselor or a trusted friend, they look over what they've written and decide what it was about those experiences that they found so energizing and memorable.

Believing as we do that God has created us to find ourselves in him and to serve him, it may be very important for women to look back and remember who they were before the culture took away their sense of their gifts and calling.

Finding Our Calling: What Do I Really Love to Do?

Many Christians believe that if something feels good it must be bad.

Sandy came to my study. She spoke hesitantly: "I'm a business major. I really hate it."

"Have you considered changing your major?" I asked perceptively.

Her whole countenance changed. "I've always loved to write. More than anything. I will sit and write for hours. And I love to read. But I never thought I was any good at it until I was in high school and my English teacher liked my poetry."

"You're a pretty outstanding writer," I said to her. "Have you considered a writing major?"

"Well, I don't know how I could. It would seem too good to be true. To major in something I like . . . it would almost seem too easy somehow."

"You know," I said, "I believe that one of the main ways that God guides us is through giving us a sense of real joy, deep joy, in something we're called to do. Most of us have in us somewhere the idea that if I really like it, it must be wrong. It's a bit warped."

Sandy's eyes got bigger. "Then you really think I could be a writing major?"

Women's situations can make them feel trapped, as if they have no choices. Many women struggle to pay attention to any feelings, let alone their gifts and callings; they may decide just to do their duty and not pay attention to what makes them feel really great.

I have friends who hate everything about speaking in front of a group, but thrive on organizing. For me to look at a stack of papers and think of working out details feels overwhelming and distressing. When I was contemplating teaching grade school I knew almost immediately that this was not my calling. (We've all known teachers who shouldn't have been.) Pursuing the wrong calling can cause terrible damage, both to the psyche of the individual who's trying to do something she wasn't called to and to those around her.

For years I had done no public speaking. There were few opportunities at a large university. When I was in seminary in England, I felt very shy because of my accent and the foreign style of verbal repartee that went on in the dining hall. I began to have the impression that I couldn't speak in public. When I was asked to read a Scripture passage at church in Cape Town, I said, "No, I'm not good in front of people."

Then I was asked to give a talk at a conference which drew from my experience of Christ. I loved working on the talk, and although I was nervous about it, I felt great while I was doing it. Afterward many people commented on the talk, and several people said to me that they thought this was perhaps a gift of mine. I felt completely energized.

Notice that there were several clues here about my gifts and calling. One was how I felt when I was preparing and giving the talk. Another was the fact that I felt energized afterward: it was not a draining experience. Also, my calling was confirmed by other people's affirmation.[8]

Finding My Calling: What Do I Feel Most Strongly About?

God may also show us our calling by directing the focus of our passions. The apostle Paul wrote, "Woe to me if I do not preach the gospel!" He felt strongly compelled, not by people pushing or shaming him, but by a burning inner desire to tell others about his Lord.

One friend has noticed that when she's in a gathering she finds herself drawn to older people. She has a special calling to them.

Another woman, a teacher, found that whenever she saw a news story or an interview about inner-city high-school students and their lives, she started to cry. The response made little sense to her. After this went on for a year or two, she met a social worker who was looking for an educator with compassion for inner-city kids. My friend's empathy was an indication of her God-given calling.

The High Cost of Calling

Okay, it's confession time. There are times when I wish I hadn't been called. I get tired. Sometimes the thought of a life of pure frivolity and fun sounds pretty appealing.

A visitor to South Africa once wrote that he would like, just for a month, the life of a rich, white South African housewife. What appealed to him was her beautiful home, swimming pool, servants, private schools for the kids, the Mercedes, the days of tennis, bridge. He thought it would be the ideal life. Occasionally I agree.

There are days when I don't want to teach students and listen to them and try to draw them further on their intellectual journeys. There are times when the project of writing a book seems overwhelmingly impossible and I want to never write another. I say to my husband, "I'm quitting."

"What are you quitting?"

"Everything. I'm going to knit."

He doesn't need to respond, because we both know that the appeal of that life, the life of the rich, white South African housewife, would last a couple of weeks and then spin off into meaninglessness, trivia, boredom and futility.

But make no mistake: calling is costly. We recognize that truth when someone is called to missionary work, when the call means extremes of climate, distance from family and difficult conditions. We salute this calling as noble. But most callings carry a high cost.

The Necessity of Pursuing Our Calling

Women need to pursue their callings for their own joy, for the blessings they will give others and because God calls them to.

What if we were judged, not only for having signed or not on a particular dotted line of faith, but for how we used our lives, how we invested the talents given to us? What would it be like if a woman were to be judged on the basis of God's call to her, rather than his call to someone else?

My two sons and I were camping near Reims and driving along on a lovely summer day through fields and vineyards when we saw a World War I cemetery. We turned in and parked. We spent perhaps an hour walking among the graves. There were lines of French soldiers—one headstone with a soldier's body stretched out in each direction from it. Next to it were the German graves. The only difference was the names. Then there were two large monumental stones with flowers around them. One read, "Here lie the bodies of 2,345 French soldiers, killed in service in the Great War." Nearby was another: "Here lie the bodies of 3,244 German soldiers, killed in service in the Great War." These had been so mangled they couldn't be identified and buried.

Staring at the graves, I thought of the countless plaques I've seen in English village squares and churches—scores of names of young men who died when people didn't even know that "the Great War" might prove to be an ambiguous term. I thought of the lists of young men from the Oxford and Cambridge colleges—bright, talented and gone. When you think of that waste—of the wonderful music they might have composed, the wonderful poems they might have written, the teaching they might have done, the medical breakthroughs—who knows what the world might have been like had they not died?

"We are horrified by the waste of war," writes Dorothy L. Sayers. "Curiously enough, we are not nearly so much horrified by the waste of peace and prosperity."9 The waste of peace is the waste of those who are not encouraged to find and use their gifts, those who are told to fritter their lives away on endless crafts and teas and tennis, rather than offering their gifts to God for the kingdom. The waste of peace is women's choosing to hide behind the roles given them because they want to be good.

"If one member suffers, all suffer," writes the apostle Paul (1 Corinthians 12:26). Yes, it's true that if one member within a healthy community suffers a devastating loss, all will feel it. And certainly if one member dies tragically young, all suffer loss of the potential of that life. But it is true too that if one member is squelched, put in the nursery because she's female when she has a gift for preaching or so disenfranchised that she leaves the church, she suffers—and all who might have benefited from her ministry suffer.

At Chartres Cathedral in France, there is an impressive tympanum over the east door, a carved arch showing the Last Judgment of Christ. The dead are judged at their deaths, and some are walking toward bliss and are being met with joy by loved ones. Others writhe toward damnation, prodded by demons.

But this tympanum also shows another judgment, the last one when Christ returns. Here the dead are being judged not only for their "saving knowledge of Jesus." They are being judged not only for the deeds they performed while they lived on earth—the "wood, hay, straw" about which Paul writes (1 Corinthians 3:12). They are being judged for the results of those deeds in future generations. In this scenario, for instance, the Nazi who killed a nameless young Jewish man is held responsible for the loss of his talent, the music he might have composed, his enthusiasm as it might have touched others.

This tympanum underlines the truth that our acts, following our callings, are of incalculable importance. We need to take seriously our gifts and callings from God; we need to pursue them as if they matter, as if the world might be changed by our obedient response to Christ. And, speaking of judgment, it is damnable when some men—frightened for their positions and jockeying for power—promote false teaching to keep "women in their place," when their place according to the practice of Jesus and Paul is using their gifts to advance the kingdom.

Or as teacher and writer Parker Palmer puts it, "Everyone has the right, perhaps even the imperative, to reach for self-expression not to gratify every whim but to serve as one who was created to serve."[10] We are called to act, but we need to make sure that we're following our calling.

"Is this vocation worth my life?" This is the question teacher/writer Mary Rose O'Reilly suggests that people need to ask themselves.[11] Consider for a moment the church's impact on the world if half of its members were set free to pursue their God-given callings as if they are worth their lives.

Part 3
Answering the
Call of Jesus:
The Balancing Act

J esus calls women to follow him. To follow, women need to grow in self-recognition and to step out of their roles. In their following, women need to commit themselves to pursuing God-given callings.

Each step of the balancing act is tricky for women, made more difficult for a number of reasons. Take women's relational lives. Women tend to value relationships more highly than men. But the domestic angel myth has told women that their relationships should be their lifework. And thus what should be a simple act on the balance beam becomes for women more like a complicated square dance: in her relational life she dances the grand-right-and-left with her children and do-si-dos with her partner, and sometimes does a solo fling on her own.

Similarly, because women have received such mixed messages about work, it is easy for them to be pulled off-balance in terms of their working lives.

The balancing act that is a woman's life is constantly challenging. Let's get practical: how do we walk the tightrope, balancing our relational lives, our parenting lives and our working lives? How do we keep following, balancing and taking risks in all the changing scenes that make up our lives?

10
Relationships
& Calling

*W*ell, if we're all pursuing our callings, who is going to look after the kids? Who is going to make sure that people are civil to each other, that thank-you notes get written? How do we maintain a balance in seeking to follow Jesus within the web of our relationships?

As I was working on this chapter, the doorbell rang. I went to the door, and there was a man whose arms were missing from the elbow down. He had hooks where hands might be. "We have a real deal going on a cord of wood, ma'am," he said. "Usually we sell for a hundred and ten a cord, but because it's late in the season, we'll give it to you for eighty-five. Guaranteed dry and red oak."

Thinking as I was about women and their sense of responsibility to others, I noticed that my thoughts were not only on the wood. I did think that maybe we would need some wood. But more of my mind wondered how he must have lost his hands, and what it would be like being in the wood business with no hands. "Yes," I said. "I'll have a cord."

When the truck came around to the back, his partner started to tell me about the special deal they could give me on two or even three cords. I thought a little about the wood, but just as much about how these guys were all out working so hard, and that it was icy and must be a real pain, and already they had cut the wood. And I thought about how lucky I was to have a great job and not have to do that kind of labor.

I know what my husband would do in a similar situation. He'd figure out if we needed wood, how much, how good the wood looked, how much it cost, and then he'd decide.

I like the fact that as a woman I see below the surface, that I consider the needs of the many people involved, that I don't see them as simply faceless workers providing for my needs. But my empathy can make it hard for me to say no. It probably makes me a sucker for all sorts of scoundrels. It makes decisions much more complicated. For me, buying wood is a moral decision, based on a constellation of issues and relationships, short-lived though they be.

This is true for women: they are different. No one can quite decide whether it's because of women's biological differences, because they are raised differently or because they are created differently by God. But it is clear from the vast majority of research that women value relationships more deeply than men do. Women regard themselves and their decisions within a web of relationships. In fact, much of the work of feminist scholars in the area of psychology over the last fifteen years has focused on women's greater affiliation tendencies. In other words, women see their lives in connection with others.[1]

Because women care so much about relationships, they often fear success, power, selfishness, anger and isolation. Women fear that their success will separate them from others, that doing well in their calling may isolate them. Women need to find balance in order to find well-being.[2]

How can a woman grow as she pursues her calling and gifts without letting go of her relational strengths?

Women's Growth in Connection

Women's primary understanding of themselves tends to be relational; that is, "the self is organized and developed in the context of important relationships."[3] Women have a wonderful capacity for empathy and for mutuality, which is an "appreciation of the wholeness of another person."[4] When a woman makes decisions, she sees their effect on a number of others; she believes they need careful consideration beyond a simple ethical formula.[5] Women feel the constant tension between being separate and being bonded; they try to fulfill both senses of responsibility—commitment to obligations and responsiveness in relationships.[6]

This can make decisions like whether or not to move extremely difficult for women. The traditional fifties man, offered a promotion that would involve his family's moving (again), saw the decision simply: The web of relationships torn? Hey, no problem, I'm being offered big money and a better job. The woman had to weigh the impact on the children and herself, with her duty to her husband.

Women often characterize their lives as being anchored by relationships. But the relational richness of women's lives can mean that they focus on relationships and lose themselves. Caught up in trying to keep everyone happy, they miss their calling and trade healthy relationships for unhealthy ones.

Women worry about relationships: they feel uncomfortable being angry, except in the service of others.[7] Practically more than anything, women fear being labeled selfish, so they experience their own "selfishness" as an act of aggression: "To act out of one's own interest and motivation is experienced as the psychic equivalent of being a destructively aggressive person."[8] Women often worry about whether they are giving enough, while research shows this doesn't enter into a man's image of himself. This is one of the reasons women have so much difficulty saying no.[9]

Even the independent woman tends to focus on others' approval, striving for affirmation and compliments. If she is sensitive, she may take to heart any perceived lack of approval. She will probably find it easier to pay attention to the needs of others than to know and express her own needs; this may make it difficult for her to separate herself even from bad relationships.[10]

Healthy Relationships: Sense of Self and Boundaries

Because of their relational affinities and empathy, women need a strong sense of self to be able to draw boundaries. How do you know if you have a boundary problem? Do you ever find yourself taking (even emotional and psychological) responsibility for something that is not your responsibility at all? Do you find yourself apologizing for something that is not your fault?

Minister's wives specialize in boundary problems. If my husband is running late for an appointment, I feel I ought to apologize. If his sermon is too long, I feel a burning responsibility in the pew. If someone criticizes his handling of something, I feel like it is my business: I must pass it along and set him straight.

Two years after we had moved from Cape Town to Minnesota, we had passed beyond the honeymoon period at our new church. I'm not sure what phase we were in, but it certainly wasn't the honeymoon, nor was it happily married. At that low time—we were struggling financially, and Ernie's gifts and ministry didn't seem to be appreciated by our local congregation or the wider church—he was offered a new job. It seemed wonderful: much more pay, a lively church, real appreciation of his gifts. We traveled to look at the church, and they gave us the five-star treatment, pleading with us to come.

Back home, we struggled to make the decision. Over the years we'd learned to make decisions together: pray, discuss the problem and agree. We discussed and discussed, and instead of coming to agreement as we had before in our lives, we moved further and further apart.

I felt that we simply could not move. It would be violating our call to Minnesota, to the people in the church; it would give a false message to the diocese. And I felt very uncomfortable with many aspects of the other church, including its conspicuous wealth and the lack of concern for workers who were lower on the totem pole. I realized, knowing my husband as well as I did, that he'd be miserable.

The job looked wonderfully appealing to him. Finally, the appreciation he deserved. But if I felt uncomfortable, then it couldn't be right. That's what Ernie said. He phoned them and told them so. A few days later he got a call back. If it was his wife who was the problem, would an extra ten thousand a year help?

Of course I was furious, and my husband turned them down again.

And for me the boundary issues really started.

Every Sunday in church I was aware that we were there because I had felt we couldn't leave. I sat in the pew, overwhelmed by all the things that would need to change for the church to grow and thrive. I noticed if Ernie's sermons were a minute too long, if his illustrations were dull, if the organ was too fast, if the ushers didn't greet people at the door. If anything wasn't quite right I got up to take care of it. I helped with the music, the Sunday school, the house groups, the healing ministry, the greeting.

With my wonderful womanly empathy, I felt every disapproving glance from a church member. I knew every tone of voice that indicated lack of approval. I felt it all keenly, and since it was my responsibility, I pointed it out to Ernie. And I was good at it. I am a terrific critic and an excellent strategic thinker, and I used all these skills to help my husband.

After church, all Ernie and I could talk about was how services could be improved. Our moods were now linked on a roller coaster of how services had gone, how things in the church were going. Our relationship was less like a marriage than a business partnership.

I was doing a great job.

But it wasn't my job.

One day it hit me. I was feeling responsible for things that were none of my business. This was Ernie's job, for heaven's sake, not mine. I could see that if I didn't get this straight now, I would be expecting the kids to be good minister's kids.

So I quit.

I decided that I would be involved in the church in much the same way any active church member would be. I would lead a house group like any other house-group leader, be involved in the drama group and go to services. Period.

It took me awhile. I had to learn to sit in a service and worship rather than criticize. I had to learn to let go. That's what my decision about boundaries was—learning to let go of that which was not my responsibility.

The liberation of letting go meant that I could begin to contemplate my own calling. Having made the decision to let Ernie do his job, I started looking at colleges where I could go back and finish my degree.

Boundaries give women the strength to say no. When a woman has boundaries, she decides what areas she wants to share with others and respects her own privacy and that of others. "This freedom to expose who we are is hand in glove with knowing what our rights are, saying yes and saying no."[11]

The boundary is "like a cocoon made of fine, strong mesh screen, encompassing and protecting our whole self."[12] The boundary helps a woman differentiate between herself and others. Despite her compelling relational skills and empathy, a woman with boundaries can figure out what things are for her to feel and do and which are for someone else. The boundary, according to Marilyn Mason, should have a zip on the inside. That means that it is the self who decides when to let others in or not.

It would be nice if we could set boundaries once and for all. I was surprised that I had to do it again later, in a new church. Once again I had to learn to say no, learn to find out how to be myself in a new situation. As I talked with my spiritual director about this challenge, she asked me a good question: "How did you become your own person when you felt this pressure before?"

I thought about it and answered, "I went back to school and went

on to do a Ph.D." I shuddered. "I don't want to have to do that again."
"You shouldn't have to do something external to say no," she said.
"You've got to find a way to do it from the inside."

Boundaries are vital: Christian women need to prioritize their lives, to leave space for their own spiritual nurture, for their personal growth.

Healthy Relationships: Support and Challenge

How can women cultivate relationships in healthy ways? How can their relationships challenge and nurture them?

Women need to put their strong affiliation tendencies to work to build a system in which they are accountable. When we choose accountability, we are choosing to go deeper, to peel back the layers. We are choosing to grow by becoming answerable to God and to others; we are putting our spiritual and emotional growth as top priority in our lives. This choice can be painful. When we are accountable we will see areas of ourselves—desires, temptations, emotions—that we'd hoped had disappeared. Accountability may involve showing weakness and being vulnerable with others. It will certainly involve gaining a clearer perspective on our lives.

When Martha approaches Jesus, she has a need for help with dinner. It's easy to be like Martha and have very little perspective on what we really need. But we can get this perspective from someone else, a trusted friend, a house-group member, a mentor, a spiritual director.

Without the help of others, we are like the blind men and the elephant, captives to our own limited perspective. Human beings have an almost infinite capacity for self-deception. The rich man in Jesus' parable has such good crops that he tears down his barns and builds bigger ones. He says to his soul, "Soul, you have ample goods laid up for many years; relax, eat, drink, be merry." What we see here is the individual's outstanding capacity to be just plain wrong. God says to him, "You fool! This very night your life is being demanded of you" (Luke 12:13-21). This rich man needed friends to whom he was accountable: "George, I'm going to be frank with you. You don't need bigger barns. You need to give the surplus away." Or perhaps a spiritual director: "George, let me tell you something you may or may not want to hear. You need to start doing things to feed your soul. What's it going to be?" The rich man needed the support and challenge of others so that he couldn't give himself a warped version of reality.

We all need people in our lives who know the worst and love us anyhow. Every individual has the right to have a place where she can be herself, says Jean Vanier, founder of the L'Arche communities, where able-bodied and severely handicapped people live together.[13] When we can be ourselves we are given God's perspective—that we are known and loved—fleshed out, in human form.

Where to Look for Accountability
Sadly, the church is often the last place where people feel they can be themselves; other Christians are the last ones we want to let our hair down around.

Whom should we be accountable to? I believe that all of us need several kinds of accountability. Some accountability is mutual, and some is not. We can assume that many marriages and friendships will be mutually accountable, but we shouldn't feel the need to ask the therapist, "And you—how was your week?"

Marriage is a wonderful place for mutual challenge and encouragement. Sometimes the radio preachers' version of marriage, however, discourages mutuality. Following the teaching of separate spheres, men and women are portrayed as having totally different needs and wants, of being such different animals as to have little common ground, except perhaps in bed. In fact a healthy marriage can be the ground for wonderful support and challenge from one whom you know loves you deeply.

My husband and I constantly challenge each other. If I feel that he's not taking enough time to listen to God, I tell him. If he's slacking on time with the family, he'll hear about it. I believe that God has given me to him to speak honestly to him.

He challenges me too. When my lack of confidence rears its ugly head, he says, "I know you can do this, Mary Ellen. You're the perfect person to speak there. I'll take care of the kids. I really think you should take this on."

At its best, marriage creates a space where growth can happen: growth through encouragement, security and challenge. But it can also be a place where partners provide unhealthy protection and enable each other's neuroses and anxieties, instead of challenging each other to grow.

And there are areas of my life where Ernie will never challenge me, because they are areas that he's not much aware of or perhaps too close to. I need others to be mutually accountable to.

Five years ago my husband and I were wrestling with a job offer. We went and saw the church and met the committee, looked at area schools and houses. Then we went on vacation . . . and guess what we talked about the whole vacation. Back and forth, back and forth— these things were positive, these were negative. It was hard for us to talk about anything else. I met with a wise friend in London, and she said to me, "You need someone else who you are regularly praying and sharing with. Ernie's great, but the two of you get too intense, especially at decision-making times."

When I got back, I phoned Megan and told her I needed to talk to her. I explained that I needed someone I could trust, who I knew would be silent about anything I said, who would pray with me. She said sure. That was five years ago, and we have met almost weekly since. We have laughed together, shed many tears together, challenged each other to grow, confessed to each other. I still do those things with my husband, but I needed someone else.

This kind of relationship may not just "happen." You will need to look at people with whom you feel comfortable and directly propose an accountable relationship, as I did with Megan.

I also believe that most of us need to belong to a small group, a Bible study or prayer group, which brings us a different kind of accountability. Clearly it is inappropriate to share your deepest, most shocking secrets with a group of people, but a group can challenge and inspire and encourage courageous acts.

With accountability it is important to keep boundary issues in mind, asking questions like "What is appropriate for me to share with whom?" More is not necessarily better. Cathartic self-revelation can be self-serving. You know the feeling of boundary violation—when it feels as if someone is telling you more or demanding more of you than you want to give or than they have the right to demand. Similarly, if you feel that you are forced in some way to share more than you are ready to, or you feel you are giving someone else more power over you than you are willing to, this is a boundary issue. We need to be aware of what is appropriate to share in given circumstances as we are seeking to be accountable.

From time to time most of us will need relationships that are not mutual, with people like mentors, counselors, pastors, spiritual directors. Any of these can be extremely helpful, partly because the relationship exists only for accountability and growth. A friend once said to me, "Going to a counselor can be the best gift you ever give yourself."

In the New Testament there are no solitary Christians. Henri Nouwen writes,

Much suffering is caused by the fear of confessing and asking forgiveness. I have seen the most radical changes in the lives of people when they finally found the courage to confess what they felt most ashamed of or most guilty about and discovered that instead of losing a friend they gained one. Distances were bridged, walls came tumbling down, and abysses were filled in.[14]

11
Motherhood
& Personhood

I was speaking at a conference in Madison, and Barbara asked if she could see me. We sat in the hotel coffee shop. Clearly, she'd been crying. "What's wrong?" I asked.

"Family problems," she said.

Oh, great, I thought, *another divorce.* "Tell me about it."

"I'm the oldest," Barbara said. "And my parents are really finding it hard to let me grow up. They were okay with college, but they think graduate school is changing me, making me disagree with them. My mom thinks I'm being rebellious when I don't ask permission to do everything.

"And now my studying biology has started to worry her. She fears that somewhere in my M.A. program I'll be forced to compromise my faith. So she keeps pleading with me to come home. When I tell her that I'm learning to be independent, that I'm growing in my faith, she just falls apart. Says I don't need to be independent. Says she went from being a daughter to a wife, and that's what I should do. I can't be that way.

"All she ever wanted to be was a mother," Barbara cried. "Or so she says. I wonder if she's pressuring me because she wishes she'd done more. I find myself planning my time too full so that even in the vacations I won't have time to go to Vermont. I'm not rebellious, but right now I wish I would never have to go home again. She makes me feel bad, like a child, like I can't do anything right."

As Barbara talked, it became clear that her mother was driving her away. Her mothering was killing her relationship with her daughter.

Called to Motherhood and Personhood

Motherhood confronts women with the most pressing challenge to keep their relational tendencies from getting out of hand. Instinctual mother feelings are very strong. These feelings are strongly reinforced by the myth of the domestic angel, which glorifies motherhood, and by so-called Christian messages that tell women that motherhood is the highest calling. These three, braided together, make a powerful rope that trips up a woman's balancing act.

No wonder we are so ambivalent about mothers. People roll their eyes when mothers are mentioned, but they madly send cards and flowers and eat brunch with mothers on Mother's Day. Women have been so pushed to make motherhood more than it should be that many children who want to honor their mothers feel oppressed by them.

Jesus had to push his own mother to follow her calling as a disciple over her role as a mother. As we have seen, Jesus' rejection of motherhood and family as the highest calling is reiterated several times in the Gospels.[1]

Many of us fall for what Mary, the mother of Jesus, was tempted to do. We are persuaded to make motherhood our career. Can we be blamed? We have been told that motherhood is the supreme career plan. But motherhood blown out of proportion can make a woman dangerous and manipulative, like Barbara's mom.

How can women get rid of the domestic angel's demands that she always be subordinated to others, without throwing the baby out with the bath water?

Motherhood Off-Balance

Mothering, like fathering, is a relationship. It is not a career. When it is elevated to the role of career, women are hurt. And children are damaged when mothers treat them like little commodities that need to perform well.

Motherhood (or fatherhood for that matter) is not a career, it is not a popularity contest, it is not even a friendship. It is a very important responsibility. The role of the parent is to create a safe place for children to grow into responsible adults. Please notice that I'm not saying that women shouldn't spend years looking after their children or that motherhood is not a crucial relationship. I believe that years spent largely looking after children are wonderful—I feel fortunate to have had all those hours in the botanical garden, at the beach, reading books and more books, biking together. I wouldn't trade those for anything. But if motherhood becomes something else—a career or a popularity contest—it tends to warp the relationship and damage the people involved.

Motherhood is a very important relationship. "To be a mother is to consider child care an important part of one's working life," writes philosopher Sara Ruddick.[2] Mothering is hard work, requiring much thought, Ruddick argues, as the "mother assumes the primary task of maintaining conditions for growth: it is the mother who considers herself and is considered by others to be primarily responsible for arrested or defective growth."[3]

As important as mothering is, the fantasy figure of the domestic angel casts a long shadow on the real mother's life, a shadow of self-doubt and guilt. It can be hard for women to remember that motherhood—important as it is—is primarily a relationship.

When Andrew was ten, he landed the part of Oliver in the musical at his school. We organized a car pool with another family for getting kids to and from the many rehearsals and performances. One day when it was our family's turn to drive, we got our wires crossed. I thought my husband was picking the children up, and he thought I was. So the three kids stood for an hour on an early fall afternoon at the school before they were picked up. When I got there I apologized to them.

That evening I got a nearly hysterical phone call from the other mother. Why hadn't they been picked up? Would this happen again? She had to know that they wouldn't be kept waiting like that again. She had felt so helpless when she'd heard they'd been kept waiting.

I was marveling on the other end of the phone. I thought to myself, *What is this about?*

Then I realized that one of the main items on this woman's job description was "Pick up children promptly after activities." For that system to have broken down meant that in some way her job was not done, that her whole life work was called into question.

The woman for whom motherhood becomes a career often will take the small items of life—getting the right healthy or homemade snacks—and blow them to enormous proportions.

Human beings, as Dorothy Sayers suggested, must have occupation; take away a woman's meaningful tasks, and she will fill her time with something else, treating the trivial as if it were of the utmost importance. If motherhood is a career, a woman approaches her children out of neediness rather than strength, and the children may feel the awful demands of being another human being's life.

Kandace talked about the terrible pressure of having this kind of mother: "When any relatives or my parents' church friends were coming over, my brothers and I started to sweat. But I think as a girl it was worse for me. I realize now that it was because someone's visit was like a performance review for my mother. Somehow I used to end up saying the wrong thing or putting my elbows on the table. Afterward my mother would tell me how ashamed she was. I learned that what was important about me had very little to do with who I was; it had more to do with how I performed for Mother."

Most of us have had the frightening experience of being at a child's soccer, basketball or baseball game and seeing parents who don't seem to care so much how their child feels as how he or she performs for them. In a basketball league my daughter was in (very briefly) some parents actually came to blows at the end of one game. There was intense competition over their alternative product lines.

Many women raised by "career mothers" feel an ongoing pressure to act happy and successful, to prove their mother's worth by being outstanding products. "In our ambitious, competitive, production-oriented society, a mother may naturally want to create a good product—to show herself, the world, and her own mother that she is a 'good mother,' that she has done her job well."[4]

When motherhood is a career, a tremendous amount of energy must be poured into it. The mother knows that this may be her little Suzy's only opportunity to learn French. We all know that after age three, second-language acquisition will never be so easy again, so the pressure is on Suzy's mom to get her French lessons; the pressure's on Suzy to learn and parrot in front of friends and relatives.

This kind of focus on children is relatively new, developed within the myth of the domestic angel. The idea of a protected childhood in which little is demanded of children except that they perform for their parents, who act as servants, social secretaries and chauffeurs, has been growing over the years.[5]

Today's mothers feel guilty if their children are not taking dance, French, gymnastics, violin, flute, pottery, art, basketball, baseball and soccer. With each of these, more money is spent, and time evaporates into driving to games, classes, meets; meals are snatched at McDonald's. Often the way children are served does not serve them well.

Motherhood Off-Balance: The Effects on Mom
Martina's twin sons left home for college, and she didn't know how to fill her time. Her life since they were born had been focused on looking after them and caring for their needs and those of her husband. She found herself wandering from room to room, picking up

a magazine and putting it down. All the things she had promised herself she would do when they left home evaporated. How could she sit down at her loom when they weren't around? She spiraled into a depression that didn't lift for months. For Martina the change in this central relationship threatened her whole sense of who she was.

For the sake of both the mother and the children, motherhood needs to be kept in its place as a crucial relationship. Psychologists suggest that for women, even the threat of a disrupted connection can be perceived not as a loss of a particular relationship but as the loss of a sense of self. Women, prone as they are to depression, feel desperate to keep their children loving them.[6]

The mid to late forties can be a crisis time for many women. Although her husband is often reaching the pinnacle of his career and the height of his productivity, the woman's life is being emptied of meaning as her children need her less and less. Because women have been asked to sacrifice their own dreams for the sake of the domestic angel myth, they are very vulnerable. Researchers have shown that the most vulnerable woman is the one who has spent her whole life at home with children, but who now must (because of divorce or college expenses, for instance) go out and get work. These women fear the job market and their own inadequacy. They fear that these new demands call into question or trivialize their choices over the years.[7]

In the balanced world where the ethic of Jesus (rather than Ruskin's separate spheres) reigned supreme, this time would not be such a crisis. From the time they were first married, both members of the couple would have pursued callings (paid or not) and would have balanced those with the demands of parenting. They would have encouraged each other to use gifts for the kingdom and to parent in a responsible manner. With the children growing up both would feel sorrow, but they would make adjustments.

Most families struggle to adjust when the children leave home. But if motherhood is a relationship, then the woman still has her relationship with the child, though it may be a long-distance one, and she has herself. Having herself, she can let her child go instead of suffocating the relationship. Because motherhood is not her career, she doesn't lose her job when her children move out.

Motherhood Off-Balance: The Effects on the Children

"So what did Sara say?" my husband asks.

"She told me that Hank came in late one night last week and told her that although he loves and respects Sara, Anne is all he's ever wanted—that Anne makes him feel special in a way that Sara never has . . . Why do men do this?" I rage. "Hank's like a big spoiled brat who wants his own way all the time. All these guys who are about forty and decide that they need a cute sweetie wife . . . Lord, deliver me from raising spoiled brats!"

A few weeks later we were visiting old friends in Washington State, Kurt and Gloria and their two sons, Brad and Frank. Gloria and I were talking.

"Mom," says Brad (age eleven), "I want something to drink."

"I made up grape juice this morning," I tell him. "It's in the refrigerator."

Brad leans over Gloria. "Mom, you know I don't like juice. Won't you get me something else?"

"There's milk . . ." I begin, but Gloria stands up. "Come on, sweetie, I'll get you something."

Ten minutes later Frank (age thirteen) comes in. "Mom, you said you'd take me to buy baseball cards. Can we go now?"

Gloria looks at her watch. "I'm not sure, honey. I promised your father that I would get him some of the socks he likes, and that I'd pick him up by five o'clock . . . and I can't be late . . ."

"But Mom, you promised."

"Well, okay. We'll run over right now, but we'll have to hurry." She grabs her bag and heads for the door.

The next morning Gloria says, "That sports store didn't have what Frank wanted, so I'll need to run to one about half an hour away, which I guess will take most of the morning. Frank doesn't really want to come, so I thought I'd drop the kids at the Y to swim on the way and then pick them up on the way back. Do we need anything for lunch?"

That afternoon as all the kids are heading out to the local beach for a swim, Gloria pulls up. "I'll take you!" she shouts to them. As she drops her shopping bags on the table, she says, "I hate to think of them walking."

That weekend shook me. I saw myself so clearly in Gloria. I have a primal longing to do for my children what they could do for themselves. I find myself longing to pick up my son's discarded towel. When my twelve-year-old asks me where the iron is, I bite back the words "I'll do it for you, sweetie."

But watching Gloria made me think about Hank. I imagine Hank's mother bringing the Kool-Aid and cookies to him in his sandbox (at age six). I see his mother (he's now ten) slipping his chicken divan onto her plate and scraping the sauce off for little Hank. I see her picking him up from Cub Scouts, hockey, Little League; I imagine her ironing his T-shirts and bringing him the math assignments that he forgot (he's thirteen).

"Do you suppose," I say to my husband, "that when little boys are waited on hand and foot, they are more likely to grow up like Hank? Maybe the main lesson Hank learned from his mother was that a woman exists solely to meet his physical and emotional needs. Wouldn't it stand to reason that if a child grows up thinking women were designed to present an ever-smiling face, cook favorite foods for boys and make no demands on men—that's what he'll expect when he's married?"

Motherhood as career does not affect only the mother. Psychologists suggest that one of the ways we raise spoiled brats is by being the self-sacrificing, self-denying mother. Women who have no sense of their own needs and calling turn all their attention to the needs and wants of others;[8] they transform their drives into the service of another's drives.[9] Women believe that others love this kind of service, but it often leads to hatred and contempt of the servant/mother.[10] It may teach boys not to care for others or themselves—they come to believe that there is a certain kind of inferior person to whom all mundane and menial tasks should fall. This mother, with the best will in the world, may teach her son to expect women to serve him. And although the son will love his mother, at another level he will come to despise her.

And when they marry, the sick system repeats itself.[11] Many sons, according to psychologist Nancy Chodorow and others, turn this ambivalence on their wives: either they become distant from them (always off at work, never emotionally available) or they become like Hank and leave their wives for someone cuter and more admiring. In the worst cases they abuse women.[12]

If Chodorow and other psychologists are right, kids like Brad and Frank may grow up and marry—probably someone like their own mother who is ever-serving, self-denying—and things will be fine. But if she begins to find a sense of herself, or if she gains weight, or her hair turns gray, or she gets sick, then Brad and Frank will have no idea what to do. Having been taught, year in and year out, that a woman should unquestioningly meet their needs, they may well go off looking for one who will.

Motherhood Balanced: The Effects on the Children

When a mother is not using her kids for her performance review, children are given more freedom to be, to pursue their own interests— to read, to make a fort, to daydream.

Annie Dillard, in her book *American Childhood*, writes about being the kind of child who was always starting a new hobby—drawing or rock collecting. One spring she spent hours staring into a microscope, and she saw an amoeba:

> Before I had watched him at all, I ran upstairs. My parents were still at table, drinking coffee. They, too, could see the famous amoeba. I told them, bursting, that he was all set up, that they should hurry before his water dried. It was the chance of a lifetime.
>
> Father had stretched out his long legs and was tilting back in his chair. Mother sat with her knees crossed, in blue slacks. . . .

Mother regarded me warmly. She gave me to understand that she was glad I had found what I had been looking for, but that she and Father were happy to sit with their coffee, and would not be coming down.

She did not say, but I understood at once, that they had their pursuits (coffee?) and I had mine. She did not say, but I began to understand then, that you do what you do out of your private passion for the thing itself.

I had essentially been handed my own life. . . . When I left the dining room that evening and started down the dark basement stairs, I had a life. . . . Anything was possible. The sky was the limit.[13]

As a mother teaches her children, she simultaneously has to give them up. In the motherhood-as-career ethic, nothing of importance can happen if the parents are not there watching it. I imagine myself as Dillard's mom: "Oh sweetie, how wonderful. Yes, let me come and see! Maybe we can find some more. Are you sure this microscope is big enough? I wonder if you'd like to take a Science Museum class on microbes. There's one on next week . . ."

Instead, Dillard's parents gave her a life.

I find that a part of me longs to keep my children young and dependent on me. My fifteen-year-old son is taking a Latin class in another part of the Twin Cities. Part of me wants to give him his wings—to give him the sense of mastery that comes from getting there on public transport on his own. Part of me wants to chauffeur him there—I want to be waiting in my car when he comes out. When he phones to tell me he's missed his bus connection and will be a bit late, I bite my tongue. I long to say, "Don't move! Let me come and rescue you." What I need to do, to give him his wings, is to say, "Thanks for letting me know. See you soon."

It's hard for me to imagine how I would negotiate these feelings if I didn't have meaningful work and a calling that demands my time and energy. I'd find it difficult to resist the urge to wait on my kids hand and foot. I'd be offering to iron for them, to make their lunches, even though I'd know I was encouraging unhealthy dependence. (There are of course times when I, as an act of love, can make a lunch or iron a shirt for the kids, just as my husband will do such things for me and I for him.) In my longing to be needed, I have to fight the part of me that wants to pick up my eighteen-year-old son's laundry and do it for him. I know it would give him all the wrong messages, but at some level I want him to need me.

Motherhood Balanced: Losing the Popularity Contest
Some years ago Callie and Anders were over for dinner, and she asked me what it was like to have a preadolescent. I answered, "It's really hard. Andrew and I have always been such good friends. His friendship is important to me, and it's hard to set limits—"

Callie interrupted me. "Never try to be your child's friend. It's the biggest mistake you can make. Try to be their parent, and later they might become your friend."

This was one of the wisest things anyone has ever said to me. I told myself that I was a parent and my job was to raise Andrew to be healthy and mature, not to make him happy and to make him like me.

Many parents try to win a popularity contest with their children, and that makes it very hard for them to parent well. Stephen Covey, author of *The Seven Habits of Highly Effective People,* writes, "Family-centered parents do not have the emotional freedom and the power to raise their children with their ultimate welfare truly in mind. If they derive their own security from the family, the need to be popular with their children may override the importance of a long-term investment in their children's growth and development."[14]

When you are involved in a popularity contest with your children, you buy them things that they ask for when it might be better for them to do without or to earn the money themselves. You give them privileges they may not be ready for so they won't be mad at you. You allow your relationship with your spouse or your friends, or with God, to suffer as you seek to please your child.

Probably all of us give our children more than is good for them. In

The Mustard Seed Conspiracy Tom Sine writes about how we Americans often give our children designer clothes, ski vacations and trips to Disney World—then are surprised that they struggle to understand the cost of Christian discipleship. As parents we must model many ideals for children: mutual respect and partnership, discipline in spending, generosity to the poor. Children must see their fathers and mothers acting as servants to each other. They must see their parents enjoying each other and putting their mutual relationship before waiting on their children. Children must be given opportunities to serve and to be responsible.

Motherhood Balanced: Giving Each Other Freedom
Feeling the strong tug of mother instinct, hearing the domestic angel's powerful propaganda and knowing the challenges of motherhood, women find it harder and harder to find words to discuss these issues, central as they are in their lives. I believe women can make a variety of healthy choices in regard to how they pursue their callings while they are mothers. But motherhood can be so emotionally loaded that women condemn those who take a different approach.

When my husband and I first arrived for our eight-year stint in South Africa, we didn't have children. One of the other ministers in our large group of churches had a very active wife and four children. Edmund and Suzanne had hired a full-time nanny to help with the children, as Suzanne was a very gifted teacher of languages and also had an active counseling and speaking ministry. The children at the time were two, four, six and eight.

I would guess that over the first couple of years we were there, ten or fifteen women took me aside to express their "concern." The children's mother (not the father, of course) was too busy. She didn't spend enough time with them. They would all grow up deeply resenting her and probably rebel against the family, and certainly against the church and against God. We should pray for them.

Perhaps these expressions of concern were meant to help me as I became a mother. But I believe they indicated the level of angst women feel when a woman takes a different approach: Suzanne might be gifted, she might try to escape the normal womanly frustrations, but her sins would catch up with her. Judgment in the form of rebellious children would be her just deserts, and I suspect that for many of my counselors it couldn't come too soon.

All these concerned parents might be surprised that Suzanne and Edmund's children—now in their twenties—haven't particularly rebelled. Several are preparing for missionary work, and they still love their mother.

Often when I speak, someone will stand up and ask me a question like this: "If you are a teacher and a writer, how do you put your children first?"

If I had more nerve and less tact, I would say to them, "To put my children first would be idolatry—bad for them and bad for me, and especially bad for my relationship with God."

What I do answer is more like this: "It's hard, I think, for all women to find ways to balance all the demands in their lives. My husband and I have quite flexible schedules so that we can be with our children. And I believe it's important for children to learn to respect me as a person, respect my calling from God. Hopefully that way they'll learn to do that with other people, including their spouses someday."

It is a great challenge to balance all the different demands and find freedom to follow Christ in our relationships, our parenting and our work.

12
Meaningful Work & Real Rest

A woman is called by God to follow, to pursue her calling in living for Jesus. Whether a woman is employed in a particularly demanding career, works part time to supplement the family budget or is a homemaker, she needs to follow the call of Jesus. She needs to say no to the many opportunities for idolatry that come her way—in the home, with her children, in her work. She needs to remain open to God's leading. The challenge of pursuing our callings and finding balance in relationships and parenting will often come to a head in pressures related to work.

Bonnie hated her job as a corporate lawyer in Boston. But the benefits were terrific, the pay was good, and she was her family's primary breadwinner. She was an excellent communicator and was highly valued by her boss and her colleagues.

When Bonnie started having nightmares that left her drained and exhausted, she decided to stop coping. She started seeing a counselor, who helped her get in touch with long-buried feelings related to her childhood experiences. Coming to terms with her parents made her feel that she could stop demanding that her two sons be her friends.

All this growth took almost a year, and Bonnie realized many things about herself. One was that although she was a good lawyer, she didn't want to do it all her life. She started getting in touch with her calling, remembering experiences that she had found satisfying as a child. She paid attention to her strong interest in issues related to South America. She paid attention to others' comments about her gifts and strengths in volunteer and church situations.

Still, it was difficult to get the nerve to step out of her job. She had to conquer a crippling lack of self-confidence. At some level, like many women, she believed that she had done so well in her present job because she had fooled her supervisors and colleagues.

She began to realize that she couldn't find a job that more fully overlapped with her calling while she was working full time at another demanding job. So she cut back, and then she quit. It was terrifying.

Bonnie wondered if she would find work. She loved working with people from Latin America, so she volunteered in a program for them. Soon the director of the program sensed her commitment and calling and offered her part-time work. Then someone else phoned and asked if she'd be interested in working with Hispanic churches. This turned into more work.

When I last talked to Bonnie, she was finding it tough to choose between several jobs in which her calling and the work overlapped. In interviews she found she had to point out to the interviewers that she wanted to set boundaries on the number of hours she worked because of family responsibilities. She was very happy to be doing work that she loved and that blessed others: this was her calling.

Work Is Complicated

I love to talk to people about their work—my hairdresser, the dental hygienist, the heart surgeon. How do you like your work? What do you and don't you like? When and how did you decide to do this kind of work? How do you get time to do this and the other things you love? How do you fit this in with your family life?

What I discover is that work is very complicated for people: their attitudes vary from "Thank goodness it's Friday" to "Thank goodness it's Monday," with every shade in between.

Work is complicated. Many workers are being asked to give more and more hours to work. Layoffs are common; insecurity fills the workplace. Researchers point out that most workers in today's work world will change jobs many times, so flexibility becomes the key.

Most of us are unclear about what work is supposed to mean in our lives. Even if we accept the idea that women as well as men have God-given callings, we may not have any idea about how those should fit in with our working lives.

Shifting Attitudes Toward Work

Yes, work is complicated. But we are also heirs to a complex variety of attitudes toward work which affect us. Let's look briefly at those.

Although the Greeks may not have said it, they held to the "Thank goodness it's Friday" approach to work. For them work was a curse, and unemployment a virtue, as public life depended on a certain number of unemployed citizens who could discuss politics. The early church respected work, as people were encouraged to earn a living. Among some in the medieval period, work came to be seen as an impediment to what was truly important—the contemplative life. Work got in the way of a proper detachment from created things and kept people from their most important job, which was getting ready to meet God. Acts of charity were a bit different because they helped you toward God, but it was clear that life at its best could be fully lived only in the cloister. The Benedictines were a clear exception to this; they believed in work, but that work was for giving more than for getting.[1]

In the Renaissance, attitudes toward work shifted again. The distant, pure intelligence that was God to the medieval mind became to the Renaissance mind the Creator, the Divine Artificer, the supreme Maker and the mightiest Architect. The call to humanity was to respond by becoming godlike not only in thinking but also in action. As people created and produced, they imitated God.

New views of work also came through the Reformation. As Luther drew a distinction between the kingdom of heaven, in which we relate to God, and the kingdom of earth, in which we relate to our neighbor, vocation came as a call to love one's neighbor. As parents, teachers and church members, Christians were called to serve others in their work.

Whereas the medieval monk chose between work that was pleasing to God or damnable, the reformed Christian saw work as a societal value that shouldn't be denigrated. To be a cobbler or a preacher was of equal value. Each person receives an individual calling—what kind of work does God want me to do?[2]

Attitudes toward work have changed. And today many people have attitudes toward work that throw them off-balance.

Off-Balance: Work Is All

From the rise of the Victorian domestic angel, men's worth was equated with their work out in the world, while their womenfolk's worth was equated with the home. The question "What do you do?" has often been answered with more of a job description than a clue about the meaning in someone's life.

Work has become more and more dominant in the lives of many people. In her book *Working Ourselves to Death,* Edith Fassell has said that work addiction is a modern epidemic;[3] people have allowed themselves to become totally enslaved by their work. They find themselves in what Juliet Schor in *The Overworked American* calls "the squirrel cage of work and spend."[4] In this cage the worker has sold out to the idea that he or she works to earn to spend. Modern advertising plays on a culture of dissatisfaction; people feel that they don't have enough or that they are deprived in some way. They work harder to buy more, and end up working frantically to support the house, the boat, the cabin, the hobby.

Even if someone works because she loves her job, it can become an idolatry. When a person needs her work to feel good about herself, when work is not just something that challenges and gives great joy but the only thing that feeds the soul, a danger alarm should sound.

Good work should make us feel involved and challenged but should not constitute our whole sense of self. If our work completely dominates our sense of who we are, we need to rethink our priorities. Perhaps we have substituted outer work for inner work on our souls.[5] If we were to pay attention to our spiritual lives and work on our relationship with God, our work might assume a proper proportion.

We've all seen workaholics—usually males, because they've had more opportunities—who give themselves only to their work, never taking time to question it, until they have a heart attack or are unable to make the adjustment to retirement. But sometimes more interesting, altruistic work is even harder to keep in perspective. We see this in ministers, surgeons, missionaries who are tempted to see their work as their whole lives. Work becomes idolatry because of the inner attitude, not the outer job description.

Olive always wanted desperately to be a writer. When her children were grown, she went back to school and got an M.F.A. in writing— at considerable financial and emotional cost.

She finished her M.F.A. and has a novel started that she really wants to finish. But it's terribly hard for her to write. Although her children are grown, other things seem to stop her from getting around to it. She feels awful about it. In fact, she feels so bad it paralyzes her.

Olive has made her work into an idolatry. It means everything to her; it defines who she is; it is her whole reason for being. Because of this, she can no longer do her work. Too much of her sense of who she is is tied up in it.

Those who have been involved in academia will recognize this syndrome: often the academic's area of expertise becomes his or her god.

Work cannot be all, or it pulls us off-balance.

Off-Balance: Lives Emptied of Work

"There can be no joy in life without joy in work," wrote Thomas Aquinas.

"Thank goodness it's Monday." Even if we can't say that, we may know what it is to enjoy the meaning and pattern that work gives our lives. Before the Fall, Adam and Eve were given work to fill their days. If our lives are empty of work, it is very difficult not to fritter away our days, wondering why we never seem to get anything done, until we've frittered away our lives.

A few summers ago I was watching my children swim at a local pool. Several other moms were sitting nearby. It was the end of August. "I went to see my doctor yesterday," said one woman. "I told him I thought I was having a nervous breakdown. I hate getting up in the morning, and then the day fritters here and there in driving and errands and kids' activities. He listened to me and said, 'Wait till the kids get back to school and you get back to work. I predict that you'll feel better.' " Many women know the end-of-summer desperate longing for some kind of routine and pattern to their lives.

Work is a great pattern-maker, giving rhythm and structure to life, making rest possible. According to philosopher Hannah Arendt, "Work and its product, the human artifact, bestow a measure of permanence and durability upon the futility of motley life and the fleeting character of human time."[6]

How would I feel if my son grew up and decided never to work? Say he simply dabbled in a few crafts, did a bit of shopping, ran errands and played golf. I'd feel it was a terrible waste. And it would be. God calls women and men to serve him, and for most of us that will mean working. Studies show that the woman who doesn't do meaningful work (paid or volunteer) becomes distracted, scattered and lost. Sometimes she becomes deeply angry and even ultimately dangerous—manipulating those she claims to love and alienating many around her. Women need creative outlets, meaningful work. Women need the joy of laboring, and then of surveying their work.

Off-Balance: Work as Curse

"Thank goodness it's Friday" summarizes many people's attitudes toward work. Work is a curse, a necessary evil that pays the bills with just enough money left over to allow them to party over the weekend or to drift into passive mindlessness—in front of a screen of some kind—in the evenings. Work is the ultimate bore. Yes, work is indeed a curse, part of the Fall of humankind in the Garden of Eden.

And yet, although people talk about their jobs as a curse, they usually don't want to quit or lose them. Often they find themselves depressed at retirement.

As we saw with Bonnie at the beginning of this chapter, the worker who hates her job can do several things. Often she can try to change what she does within the company so that her work becomes more interesting and meaningful. Perhaps she can find ways to see her work as a part of some larger plan. (For instance, many students work at boring jobs to pay for tuition so that they won't always work at boring jobs—this is taking the long view.) Sometimes a woman may find ways to enjoy her work more by focusing on parts that she likes or trying to improve certain skills. Occasionally a woman may find that she simply needs to pour herself into a calling outside of her working hours and allow her commitment to that to carry her through her work.

All jobs are boring sometimes. But if a job is boring more than 25 percent of the time, career counselors suggest that the worker should look for a way to move out of it. Is there a way to change the job? Or should I look for a new job?

Sometimes work is worse than boring; it is soul-destroying. As we saw with Bonnie, one of the reasons people hate their work is because it doesn't equate with their calling. At that point a person may need to quit.

A woman wrote to a consultant, explaining that she was in her late forties and had always hated her job. She dreamed of becoming a speech therapist and was contemplating going back to school. Her concern was that she would need to use her retirement funds to pay for schooling. Should she do it or not?

The consultant's answer was unequivocal: "Not on your life. To move out of a secure position at your stage of life would be extremely risky."

This woman is asking the wrong person, I thought. I imagine her day by day and into years, still going to that job she hates, as the dream of another calling fades from her mind, in this, her one life.

Sometimes we need support to take the risks that are necessary to follow our callings in spite of our work.

For eight years I was in a home group with about sixteen people. During that time a number of group members quit their jobs, and we thought it was a coincidence. We thought maybe we should warn new members, "Join this group and quit your job."

But I began to realize that it wasn't coincidence. In our group we prayed, worshiped, studied the Bible and shared together, and the group provided a way to think about our lives and callings. We got perspective and pondered work in the context of our overall life goals and the calling of Jesus. A lawyer quit her job; a waitress; a salesperson; a teacher; an office administrator.

Each got support to take a risk, which may have been exactly what they needed. While society said to them, "Be careful; don't take risks. What if you can never buy a boat? What if you can't get the down payment on the house?" the group said to them, "It's your life. You're better than that. You could get a job that would suit you better."

There was one person in the group, a high-powered department head in a big company, whom we knew would never quit. She had hung in there for twenty-five years, as her section had shrunk from twenty-seven employees to four.

She was about to go out of town to a conference when she was told that she needed to make another staff cut, down to two. She asked the home group for prayer and went to her conference. While she was there she prayed and realized what she should do. She came back and handed her list of cuts to her boss. Her name was on the list.

That's freedom. The free person is able to quit a job or get a job. We serve One whom to serve is perfect freedom.

On Balance: Work as Part of God's Plan

Work is not just a way to earn a buck. It is "a creative activity undertaken for the love of the work itself" so that humanity can follow the divine Creator in the joy of creation. Adam and Eve worked in the Garden of Eden. Work is part of God's intention. "Even in an ideal world, it seems, God expected us to participate in the co-creation of the world."[7] In our examination of the idea of "flow" we have seen that the worker who is caught up in what she is doing is happiest.[8]

For the Christian, "work is not a nuisance to be avoided. Work is a gift to be given," writes Joan Chittister.[9] Work offers us gifts. Not only are we able to give to the world, but work keeps us from becoming totally self-centered. Work gives us a part in the redeeming of the world and helps to build community. Work brings us self-fulfillment and also discipline, which makes us more holy. And work means that we do not live off the poor.[10]

To be Christian doesn't mean our work needs to be religious, but it must be good work, done well. "No crooked table-legs or ill-fitting drawers ever, I dare swear, came out of the carpenter's shop at Nazareth. Nor, if they did, could any one believe that they were made by the same hand that made heaven and earth. No piety in the worker will compensate for work that is not true to itself; for any work that is untrue to its own technique is a living lie."[11]

When the Lord spoke to the people of Israel about work, he said, "Six days you will labor and do your work."[12] We are called to do good work, meaningful work. We are called to make our lives count.

At its best, work provides an opportunity for self-expression, social relatedness and improving the world.[13] The joy of good work well done can put us in touch with the Creator himself.

But work becomes a gift for both the worker and the one who is at the receiving end of the work. Think of the people who have changed your life, whom you listed in the chapter on calling. Chances are that someone on your list was following their calling through their work. The worker—fully involved, giving herself to the work—blesses herself, and she blesses others. She has been blessed to be a blessing.

Sabbath

We need to take our work seriously, doing our best work for God. But God gave his people an example to help keep our work in perspective: God took a day off after creating the world. Jesus pursued his calling for thirty-three years, and then he handed the work over to others. Similarly, we workers are given the gift of sabbath, whereby we rest and restore our souls. Joan Chittister, in her book *Wisdom Distilled from the Daily,* suggests that we need rest and sabbath so that we can have a proper perspective on our work, to check whether our lives have meaning, to ask why we are doing what we are doing.[14]

Ultimately we will leave our work. The results are up to God, not us. This is the freedom of sabbath. If someone is unable to take a sabbath—a day per week of complete rest—it is a pretty good indication that their lives are unbalanced.

Chris was a very courageous woman. She had been a physical therapist and decided when she was forty that she wanted to become a doctor. She went back to school and worked very hard on her medical degree. But on Sundays she could be found swimming, walking, digging in the garden or worshiping. "My classmates think I'm nuts," she said. "They work all day Sunday. But I believe I'm called, and I'm trusting that as I rest and give this day to God, God will bless it." She passed her program with flying colors.

Psalm 90 is a wonderful reminder that God takes the long view, and that we should too. The psalmist recognizes that God is much bigger than we can fathom, that our sense of time is limited. Our days "are soon gone, and we fly away." In the light of that perspective, the psalmist asks God to "teach us to count our days that we may gain a wise heart." We are to use our days in responsible dependence, but ultimately we can only commit our efforts to God, asking him to "prosper for us the work of our hands—O prosper the work of our hands!"

Sabbath is essentially about taking the long view. It is about acting on our responsibility—six days shalt thou labor—and then handing over to God: "O prosper the work of our hands!" It is the perspective we need to take our sense of calling with us through all the changing scenes of life.

13
Through All
the Changing
Scenes of Life

Now as they went on their way, he entered a certain village, where a woman named Martha welcomed him into her home. She had a sister named Mary, who sat at the Lord's feet and listened to what he was saying. But Martha was distracted by her many tasks; so she came to him and asked, "Lord, do you not care that my sister has left me to do all the work by myself? Tell her then to help me." But the Lord answered her, "Martha, Martha, you are worried and distracted by many things; there is need of only one thing. Mary has chosen the better part, which will not be taken away from her."
LUKE 10:38-42

Charity has her act together. Okay, no one has her act completely together, but of all the people I know she has her act together most. She has a couple of kids; she doesn't work for money but is active in leadership roles in a church, challenging volunteer work with a charitable foundation and a group that works with inner-city kids. She practices hospitality, and she pursues interests in reading and writing. I love the way she enjoys life. If I phone her at seven in the evening and say, "The moon is full. Let's go cross-country skiing," she'll say, "It'll take me ten minutes to get the kids organized and I'll be over."

"What's your secret?" I ask her. "How do you have it together so well?"

"Prayer," she answers. "It's as simple as that. And I know I'm loved."

What could be more simple?

Charity's response reminds me of Martha and Mary. Mary comes to God in trust and dependence; she knows the love of God. Mary and Charity have chosen the "better part."

How do we do this over the years in the balancing act we call life?

Learning to Follow, to Say Yes and No

To maintain balance, women need to learn to say yes or no. After her revelation in the living room, Martha must have learned that she could say yes to Jesus, but she would have to learn to say no to cordon bleu.

Women learn from childhood that they should always make everyone happy all the time. This of course involves saying yes to all requests. If a woman says no she should feel really bad. With this system, most women feel that they're letting someone down all the time.

As a woman grows in balance, she learns to say no to certain demands and yes to others. Too many things come to us like Overnight Express packages. They are marked in huge letters "Extremely Urgent." I imagine myself saying to the UPS guy, "Yeah, yeah, I can see it's extremely urgent. But is it important?" He couldn't tell me, of course. That's what I've got to figure out. What's urgent, and what's important—these are questions we face daily.

A woman I know feels called to write, but she cannot earn her living writing. So she has said no to stimulating paid work and instead waits tables in a restaurant so that she will be able to have creative energy for her mornings of writing. She says no and yes with care, so that she will not be scattered in a number of directions.

People need to learn to say yes to things that promote their calling and no to things that don't. If my teacher Mrs. Holzer had not said no to full-time homemaking, she would not have been able to say yes to being my teacher. If my spiritual director had not said no to a hundred other things she could have done, she would not have been able to say a resounding yes to her calling.

In 1992 my husband wanted a new challenge, and we moved from a church where we had been for ten years to another church. Because we moved just across town, I still had friends and contacts at the old church. Many people at the new church of course wanted to get to know us. Ernie was short-staffed, and the church wanted house groups, so I agreed to run a training course for house-group leaders. I was asked to lead the women's retreat that spring and to speak at the women's group. All at the same time I was moving, helping the children settle into a new church, teaching almost full time, defending my dissertation and working on a book. Things were crazy in the choir, so I felt I should join, and a group of people interested in drama asked me to teach a class and lead that group.

I began to find life stressful. When I went grocery shopping I would run into people from the new church and feel terrible that I couldn't remember their names. People would drop over, and I didn't know what to say to them.

I went to see my spiritual director. I told her how my life felt out of control. "I cannot do everything!" I said. "I'm beginning to hate everything." She asked me what I was doing, and when I told her, she could understand my feeling overwhelmed.

"So who says you have to do all this stuff?" she asked.

"Well, there are some things you just have to do," I said. "I can't let Ernie down by not training the house-group leaders, and when that guy from England came over needing a place to spend the night, I felt I couldn't say no, and the staff Epiphany Party has been a long-standing tradition, and my daughter really wants me to go and help with her skating . . . There are some things you just have to do. Don't you believe that? That there are some things you just do, whether you like it or not?"

"I think there are a few," she said. "Very few."

I started to defend myself. "But if I didn't—"

"Are you saying you don't believe that God has gifted a number of people in your church and your family? Are you saying that if you don't do it, God has no other way to get it done?"

I thought about that for a few minutes. "I guess I am."

"If you don't say no to what is not yours to do, you won't be able to say yes to what is yours to do. You will suffer tremendous frustration trying to do a job that isn't yours. And someone else won't be able to say yes to what is theirs to do."

Purposefully, intentionally saying yes and no means learning to focus on what I've been called to do and learning to do what Dorothy L. Sayers would call my "proper job." This requires attention, much more attention than I expected. I think of myself as quite a sensitive person, but it took me months to learn to pay attention to my feelings—to notice when I said yes to something and felt low or down or drained afterward. I would complain about my teaching load and then realize that my teaching energizes me, but that I needed to drop the choir. To do my proper job, to follow my calling, I need focus, not distraction.

My spiritual director was right: if I say yes to too many things, I'm depriving someone else of doing their "proper job." By learning to focus I have allowed my husband to begin really sharing parenting responsibilities.

My friend Tony says that she cannot work outside the home, though she'd love to, because it's too hectic with the kids and because her husband works such long hours. I tell her that maybe if she didn't do it all, if she told him when *he* could pick up the kids, he'd change his way of operating. It would enrich his life as well.

As a busy minister, my husband can always find something to do. It's good for him to say, "I'm sorry, but it's my afternoon with the children." He's also discovered that he really enjoys cooking. My saying no has meant a yes for my husband. He cannot be the absent fifties dad he might have been.

Opening and Closing Doors
Looking back on their lives, most people can see moments when un-

expected doors opened before them, and when other doors closed. Because we know the grace of God, we believe that God is behind these "coincidences." But there are times when open doors represent for us not a calling but a distraction from our calling. Two doors, or more, are open and seem to have good possibilities behind them. For Martha, the door to the living room where Jesus was teaching was open. So was the kitchen door, telling her to get dinner ready and pursue something she knew she was good at.

As we grow in our self-recognition and our sense of our calling, we will be able to discern more clearly the right steps to take to follow Christ. And we will learn to say no to the wrong ones.

When I was first a graduate student and teacher, I wondered whether I should apply for a job training new writing teachers at the University of Minnesota. I knew I could do the job well, that it would give me good experience and look great on my résumé. At the same time I felt a little uncomfortable about it, and I couldn't put a finger on why.

So I went to talk to Nan, who had helped steer me toward graduate study. She listened to me and asked a few questions about how I felt about the job, my gifts, my future. "Yes," I replied, "it would involve a considerable amount of administration, which I don't like, but it might be good experience for me . . . No, I don't feel a really all-out enthusiasm about it."

She listened and thought for a while. "I wouldn't do it," she said. "My sense is that you are free to do it or not. But any door you open and go through leads you inevitably in one particular direction. It may not be a bad direction. But in my experience, any step you take moves you toward one thing and away from something else. You could always get back and go in another direction, but you may find that it takes you longer. Unless your heart is really pulling you, I wouldn't do it." I turned down the job and was very glad I had.

Maybe the reason it has taken me longer than most to learn to listen to my feelings is that during my early years as a Christian I had a very warped idea of God. In my view the Holy Spirit offered no comfort or wisdom: the Spirit operated only to convict me of sin, or maybe to help me read the Scriptures.

But my warped view of God especially affected my idea of God's guidance, which I saw as a stumble in the dark. Worse yet, the stumble was along a knife-edged clifftop with canyons on either side. My job (seeking God's will) was to try to stay on this precipice by being in the right place at the right time and never doing the wrong thing. If I was ever not in the right place, my whole life could be ruined. After that, it was God's second-best for me—I'd missed my chance. No wonder I was frightened a lot, having made God into my own mental image of a mean and arbitrary parent.

The Bible really speaks of exactly the opposite kind of God—one who, like a good parent or friend, wants to show us the way, wants to walk with us, wants to help us find ways to use our gifts and grow, one who gently closes and opens doors, one who lovingly restores us after we fall. "The human mind plans the way, but the LORD directs the steps" (Proverbs 16:9). This proverb underlines my experience over a number of years of walking with the Lord as a collaborative and cooperative experience. I bring the best plans I can make given my gifts and talents, my desires, my sense of God's strategy for my life—but it is the Lord who closes doors that seem to be open; it is the Lord who opens doors that I had no idea even existed.

Nan's advice to me was sound. Such is God's grace, that none of our steps are irrevocable; God can turn even our mistakes into wonderful new possibilities. But each step is a step in a particular direction. It is important to follow God's gracious leading, which may well come to us in the form of the peace of God acting as the arbiter, or judge, in our hearts (Colossians 3:15).

Often as we are learning to know ourselves and our gifts, we will need the counsel of others to help us. Especially for women, with low levels of self-confidence and high levels of duty, it can be easy to say yes to what seems safe and no to new risks.

To Take Risks
Jesus calls us to leave our security, to be pulled out of our comfort

zones. To set aside our security, to climb out of the boat, will look different for each of us. The risks we take are an act of faith.

The call of Jesus is a call to not get stuck, but to keep growing for life. The women whom Jesus called in the Gospels must have been shocked to have this rabbi calling them to growth and discipleship. They were called to take enormous risks.

It can be hard for women to choose growth. Psychologist Ruthellen Josselson studied hundreds of women and their life decisions, and she calls women who get stuck "foreclosures," because they are characterized by a lack of desire to grow and a lack of any sense of adventure. They are afraid to rock the boat or express frustration about their lives; usually they have little peer support to help challenge them.[1] In Josselson's study, women who kept growing were more flexible; those who had "foreclosed" on their lives couldn't bear uncertainty and risk. (The other main quality of the "foreclosures," it's sad to say, was very high levels of religiosity. It's not hard to see that this is the religion of the Pharisees, not of Jesus.)

Jesus' mother Mary must have been a strong and courageous teenager to say yes to the angel and face the sneers of neighbors. She knew how to ignore the voice of fear within telling her to play it safe, and instead to take the most extraordinary risk of saying yes to God.

But some thirty years later Mary seems to have gotten stuck. She had mothering down to an art. Just look at how great her son had turned out. He was having a terrific ministry. But Mary needed to take a new and risky step. She needed to put motherhood behind her and follow Jesus as a disciple.

Jesus loved her, and he pushed her. While he was preaching to a crowd, someone called to him, "Your mother and your brothers and sisters are here." Imagine Mary's shock when Jesus looked at the strangers around him and said: "Here are my mother and my brothers! Whoever does the will of God is my brother and sister and mother" (Mark 3:32-35).

How painful for your son to force you out of your comfort zone, and in public! Jesus would not even allow his own mother to stop growing. He pushed her to deeper discipleship, and she responded by following. Mary was there at the cross, and she was praying when the Spirit came at Pentecost. She took the risk.

The challenging Spirit of God: why should Mary be forced to be a disciple? His own mother—why couldn't he leave her alone—let her be just a mom?

"Do not be afraid." Jesus repeats these words again and again in the Gospels. When Jesus walks on the water out to where some of his disciples are in a boat, he says, "It is I. Do not be afraid."

Sitting in many pews today, you would think that Jesus had shouted constantly, "Watch out. Be careful. The slippery slope is right ahead." Plenty of preachers will tell women to play it safe, saying, "Be careful. You could hurt yourself; you could hurt your family. I wouldn't try that if I were you." Women hear this voice frightening them more than they hear the genuine voice of Jesus.

Women may prefer to listen to such voices so that they won't be challenged to step out. Or we may choose to surround ourselves with other people who we know won't question us—people who will tell us what we hope to be true. Instead we need people who will challenge us to step out of the boat, to take risks.

I recently saw a cross-stitched wall plaque behind a woman's desk. It showed a cat stuck in a net, and it read, "It's easier to get into things than it is to get out." *What a motto,* I thought. It might as well have said, "Be careful, play it safe. Don't ever try anything new."

The call to fear, the call to be careful, is the call to waste a life, to bury one's talent in the ground. Remember that story? The landlord does not say to the one who buried the talent, "Hey, no problem. You got a bit nervous." Instead he calls the man worthless, wicked and lazy (Matthew 25:26-30) for being unwilling to take risks.

Jesus knew what it was to have people tell him to play it safe. When he told his disciples that he would go to Jerusalem and be killed, Peter offered excellent advice. Essentially he told Jesus to be careful and not to do anything dangerous. Jesus rebuked him: "Get behind me, Satan. . . . For you are setting your mind not on divine things but on human things" (Matthew 16:23).

We need to learn to say to those who tell us to play it safe, "Get behind me, Satan." That voice that tells us to be careful is the voice of the devil. The powers of evil love to freeze people by fear; they love to scare women so that over half of God's church can be paralyzed into passivity.

To Never Stop Growing

Kim told me about her mother's death. "She had cancer, but she was pretty peaceful. The only thing that was really hard for her was when she suddenly realized that she had wasted her life.

"She knew she'd raised three good children, but it hit her in those last few months that it wasn't enough. She'd had her own gifts, her own calling, and she'd listened to people telling her that to raise children was all she needed to do.

"It was pretty awful. Whenever she'd think about it, she'd start to cry. The peace of her death . . . was covered with a terrible, irretrievable regret. She seemed to see it so clearly then. She'd wasted her life."

The most fearful women are those who are desperately afraid they have wasted their lives.

People are often mystified by the fact that the strongest voices against the women's movement and women's ordination (and, early in the twentieth century, against women's getting the vote) are the voices of women. Gifted preacher Brenda Salter-McNeil says that when she gets up to preach, sometimes people walk out to protest a woman preacher. Most who walk out are women. Of course they are. If God could call a woman out of the nursery and into a pulpit, anything could happen! If a woman whose life has been modeled on the domestic angel myth hears a woman preach and preach well, it calls into question her whole life. Perhaps she could have been a preacher. Or she might have become the nurse she wanted to be. Her world tips crazily. The domestic angel myth, with all its clear categories and its duties, seems for a minute like a mirage. Perhaps she has poured out her life not really following God after all. A fear grips her. The question begins to form in her mind: *What if . . . ?* She reaches for her purse. She gathers her righteous indignation around her and walks out. "Women preachers!"

It's seldom too late for women to choose to grow and follow their calling.

Pacem in Terris is a wonderful retreat center that allows many people (including me) to sit at the feet of Jesus. It was founded by a woman named Shirley Wanchena, whose husband died after they'd raised six children.

Shirley didn't sit back and put her feet up. "I thought I had enough life left to make a difference," she says, and she did. She bought land in rural Minnesota and built at first three and now nine tiny cabins, called hermitages. She welcomes guests, gives each "hermit" a basket of bread and fruit, and shows them the place where they will sit and pray and read the Bible and listen to God's voice. She asks if there are particular things she can pray for you about during your thirty-six-hour stay. The peace and solitude of this place have been a tremendous gift to me. I'm so glad Shirley knew it was not too late to say yes to God's calling to her.

"Resist doing things which have no meaning for life," said cellist Pablo Casals. Assuming we have only one chance at life, at each year, each month, each day, each hour—what things do we need to say no to, and what things do we need to say yes to? How can we get in touch with the things that have meaning for life—our lives and the lives of those around us?

Stop for a few minutes and make a list of things that you spend most of your time doing. Then circle those that make you raise the question *Does this task have any real meaning for my life?*

The Call to Maintain Balance

We women want to live real lives. We want to find a balance that we feel has often been lacking in men's lives, and in lives dictated by myths of the superwoman or the domestic angel. The compartments of men's lives—work here and home there—we don't want them. We want integration, not disintegration.

Christian women want to pursue their calling and have healthy relationships, and they want this balance to be deeply grounded in their relationship with God.[2] They want to pursue their callings without using their work to feed their souls. They want the "better part," the perspective that comes from knowing they are loved of God.

We are so easily swept into performing, as if our worth were dependent on our actions. We forget that men have tried this with jobs and accomplishments and women with their homes and families, without satisfaction. The kind of satisfaction Martha was desperate for comes only from following Jesus. He says, "Let anyone who is thirsty come to me, and let the one who believes in me drink. As the scripture has said, 'Out of the believer's heart shall flow rivers of living water' " (John 7:37-38). We come to Jesus, thirsty, and then drink. It is only out of that fullness that our lives can overflow. If we don't get the water from Jesus, we end up pumping—into our callings or our relationships—from an empty well. And it makes us unhappy and resentful. "Resentment is a signal that our service has become contaminated by sacrifice, to the detriment of everyone involved."[3]

Following Jesus and resting in his love rather than trying to prove something to God or each other or ourselves takes constant spiritual vigilance. If we find ourselves desperate for compliments—about our children, our cooking or our books—it's time to look within. During our lives, we are not either Mary or Martha. Most of us tend to slip back into being Martha—worried and distracted. We struggle to be Mary, who focused on following Jesus.

I am most easily tripped in my balancing act when I forget that I am loved by God.

For a period of time I know the "one thing" that Mary had: my central focus is God, and what I do comes out of that relationship and God's gracious love. Then, a month or two later, I realize I'm feeling frazzled and out of sorts. Like Martha, I'm worried and distracted with many things. I feel a tremendous responsibility to make everything work out well. But I can't decide whether to say yes or no: if

I don't speak to this group, who will?

Then I realize that I've done it again. I've allowed what I do to take center stage. Somehow I've pushed God off to the side; I've lost my focus. Instead of being nurtured by God's love and producing fruit, I'm madly trying to make some really great fruit so that God will love me and everyone will like me. I slip from one to the other without even noticing. I pray that I may someday come to a point where I notice when this is actually happening, rather than weeks later.

To someone watching me from outside, I might seem very much the same person in either of these two states. But in reality, in terms of what's going on within, these two inward states are poles apart, opposites—like Martha and Mary. In one I'm trying to earn God's love, and in the other I'm reveling in it.

Mary chooses the better part. She knows she is loved, and so she doesn't have to pour herself into relationships, desperately pursue career success or frantically try to be the perfect domestic angel. To be able to sit at the Lord's feet, Martha needed to be able to let go of trying to prove herself. She needed to collapse at the Lord's feet and revel in his love, get perspective and then, with this new focus, get up refreshed. It is only in knowing the love of Jesus this way that women can find the freedom to balance our lives as we follow him.

Questions for Group Study

I suggest that you read a chapter and answer any questions contained in it. Then before you meet to discuss the chapter, look at the corresponding questions listed here and think about your answers to them. Your group facilitator can decide which questions to use for discussion.

Chapter 1: The Call of Jesus to Follow

1. Read the passage about Mary and Martha aloud (Luke 10:38-42). If you had to characterize yourself as one or the other, which would you be?

2. What are some of the more Martha-like tasks in your life?

3. What are some of the more Mary-like times in your life?

4. Do you ever find yourself pigeonholing people? Are they people of a particular kind? Do you know why you do this?

5. There are times when we simply have to do things. Can you think of a time when you've done something good for the wrong reasons? How do you deal with issues of motive—what things you do and why you do them?

Chapter 2: Piecing Together a Godly Life

1. Think of your life as a quilt. What materials are you using to piece your quilt together? What parts of your quilt do you really like? What

parts would you like to unpick?

2. Why do you believe that women are prone toward losing a sense of themselves?

3. Have you ever had a sense of losing yourself in the demands on your life? What did you do about it? What would you like to do about it?

Chapter 3: Saying No to Superwoman

1. Have you felt the call to be a superwoman? How did you respond?

2. In your opinion, what good things has the women's movement done for women? What bad things?

3. Do you agree that the superwoman is dead?

Chapter 4: Saying No to the Domestic Angel

1. Share your list of what a really good woman is like.

2. What qualities of this woman have most haunted you personally?

3. If you have memories of the 1950s, what stands out?

4. What things still appeal to you about that period? What things are you thankful are long gone?

Chapter 5: Saying No to the Christian Domestic Angel

1. What qualities could you add to the list of what the really good woman is like, to make her a Christian domestic angel?

2. How has this Christian domestic angel myth affected you personally?

3. What parts of the domestic angel are worth keeping, and what parts should be thrown away?

Chapter 6: Becoming a Mature Disciple

1. Are there times when you find it hard to "grow up," when you'd rather remain like a child, or you feel like a child?

2. Do you ever find yourself "majoring on the minors," putting far more energy into something than it deserves? Give an example or two. Why do you think you do that?

3. Do you ever feel that others don't adequately value your time?

4. Do you find it difficult to value your own time? How might you change that?

Chapter 7: Unmasking Our Identity

1. Do you ever find yourself avoiding your strong feelings? Do you think that you are sometimes afraid to feel what you feel? Be specific.
2. Do you worry about being selfish or self-indulgent? When and why?
3. Are there times when you've been aware that you are seeing yourself from the outside?
4. Share your answers about what you think would make God love you more. Why do you think you struggle to believe that God loves you?

Chapter 8: Stepping out of Roles & off the Pedestal

1. Share your answer to the question "Who am I?" Were you at all surprised at what you concluded? What would you like to be able to put on a label in answer to this question?
2. Have you ever felt that you've been put on a pedestal? When and why? How did that feel? How did you respond?
3. How do you protect yourself from the grace of God? Are you a good coper? What could you stop coping with?

Chapter 9: Finding Our God-Given Calling

1. Describe one or two of the people you listed who had a major impact on your life.
2. Tell about a time when you felt happiest, when you experienced what is characterized as "flow."
3. Do the exercise described on page 109. Share one with the group. Help each other figure out what was at the heart of this experience.
4. What areas do you find you feel most strongly about? What might your feelings be saying to you about your calling?
5. Do you have a clear sense of your calling? How would you answer the question "Is this vocation worth my life?"

Chapter 10: Relationships & Calling

1. In what relationships do you find yourself most likely to have boundary problems?
2. To whom do you turn if you just want to talk? If you need a talking-to, who will give it to you?
3. Let's say you start having doubts about your Christian faith. Whom will you turn to?
4. Are there some issues in your life that you don't talk to anyone about?
5. Have you been in a situation where you felt you were accountable in the best sense of that word? Where was it, and what made it good? What do you think stops you from being more accountable to others? What steps could you take to become more accountable in your life?

Chapter 11: Motherhood & Personhood

1. Have you ever been tempted to make motherhood your career? How did it affect you?
2. Do you sometimes feel pressure to be popular with your children? How could you respond to that?
3. If a brand-new mother came to you asking for advice about the role of mothering in her life, what would you say to her?

Chapter 12: Meaningful Work & Real Rest

1. Share a high point and a low point in your working life.
2. On a continuum from "Thank goodness it's Friday" to "Thank goodness it's Monday," where would you be?
3. Have you ever found yourself unbalanced in your work?
4. How much do your work and your calling overlap? Could you make them overlap more? How?

Chapter 13: Through All the Changing Scenes of Life

1. Describe an area in your life in which you need more focus and less distraction, where you need to learn to say no to some things and yes to others.

2. What risks is God calling you to take?

3. Do you spend much of your time doing things "that have no meaning for life"? How can you "resist doing things that have no meaning for life"?

4. Do you ever feel that you're performing to earn approval? How can you find ways to rest in the love of God, to sit at Jesus' feet?

Notes

Chapter 2: Piecing Together a Godly Life
[1]Frederick Buechner, quoted in Robert Bence, *Ordinary Saints: An Introduction to the Christian Life* (Philadelphia: Fortress, 1988), p. 106.
[2]Robert Bellah et al., *Habits of the Heart: Individualism and Commitment in American Life* (New York: Harper & Row, 1985), p. 69.
[3]Alasdair MacIntyre, *After Virtue* (South Bend, Ind.: University of Notre Dame Press, 1987), chap. 10.
[4]Bellah, *Habits of the Heart*, p. 69.
[5]Robert C. Roberts, "Psychobabble: A Guide for Perplexed Christians in an Age of Therapies," *Christianity Today*, May 16, 1994, p. 18.

Chapter 3: Saying No to Superwoman
[1]Mary Stewart Van Leeuwen, review of *Who Stole Feminism? How Women Have Betrayed Women*, by Christina Hoff Sommers, *Christianity Today*, October 24, 1994, p. 102.
[2]Sylvia Ann Hewlett, *A Lesser Life: The Myth of Women's Liberation in America* (New York: Warner, 1987), p. 14.
[3]Marilyn Mason, *Making Our Lives Our Own* (San Francisco: Harper, 1991), p. 105.
[4]Arlene Rossen, *Sequencing—Having It All but Not All at Once: A New Solution for Women Who Want Marriage, Career and Family* (New York: Atheneum, 1986), p. 17.
[5]Hewlett, *Lesser Life*, p. 15.

Chapter 4: Saying No to the Domestic Angel
[1]Dorothy L. Sayers, "Are Women Human?" in *Are Women Human?* (Grand

Rapids, Mich.: Eerdmans, 1971), pp. 24-25.

[2]Stephanie Coontz, *The Way We Never Were* (New York: HarperCollins, 1992), p. 156.

[3]Walter Houghton, *The Victorian Frame of Mind* (New Haven, Conn.: Yale University Press, 1963), pp. 54-57.

[4]Deborah Gorham, *The Victorian Girl and the Feminine Ideal* (Bloomington: Indiana University Press, 1992), p. 4.

[5]Janet Murray, *Strong-Minded Women and Other Lost Voices from Nineteenth Century England* (New York: Pantheon, 1982), p. 9.

[6]Ibid.

[7]Jane Lewis, *Labor and Love: Women's Experience of Home and Family, 1850-1940* (Oxford: Basil Blackwell, 1987), p. 2.

[8]Coventry Patmore, *The Angel in the House* (London: J. W. Packer, 1854).

[9]John Ruskin, "Of Queen's Garden," in *Essays and Letters Selected from the Writings of John Ruskin,* edited by Mrs. Louis G. Hufford (Boston: Winn, 1894), pp. 81-82.

[10]Ibid., p. 83.

[11]Ibid., p. 99.

[12]In the early twentieth century Virginia Woolf wrote about this angel in one of her essays: "She was intensely sympathetic. She was immensely charming. She was utterly unselfish. She excelled in the difficult arts of family life. She sacrificed herself daily. If there was chicken, she took the leg; if there was a draught she sat in it—in short she was so constituted that she never had a mind or a wish of her own, but preferred to sympathize always with the minds and wishes of others. Above all—I need not say it—she was pure. Her purity was supposed to be her chief beauty—her blushes, her great grace. In those days—the last of Queen Victoria—every house had its Angel" ("Professions for Women," in *Death of the Moth and Other Essays* [New York: Harcourt Brace Jovanovich, 1942], p. 425). Woolf killed the angel, she says, by throwing an inkpot at her.

[13]Hewlett, *Lesser Life,* pp. 234-35.

[14]Sayers, "Are Women Human?" p. 23.

[15]Alice Kessler-Harris, *Women Have Always Worked* (New York: McGraw-Hill, 1981), p. 67.

[16]In 1850's New York, one-quarter to one-third of Irish wives took in boarders. In a study of Homestead, Pennsylvania, 40 percent of families had at least one boarder. Since a boarder's payment might add 25 percent to the family's income, women who took in paying guests could help their families survive financially without having to send children away, especially if the mother was pregnant. While the practice helped money matters, it caused

other problems, such as exposing the family members to drunkenness and even sexual abuse, when young girls were being raised in overcrowded conditions with strange men (ibid., pp. 48-49).

[17]Dorothy L. Sayers, "The Not-Quite-Human Human," in *Are Women Human?* (Grand Rapids, Mich.: Eerdmans, 1971), p. 43.

[18]Coontz, *Way We Never Were,* p. 27.

[19]Hewlett, *Lesser Life,* p. 228.

[20]Women (since the rise of the field of home economics around the turn of the century) were encouraged to treat their homemaking as a scientific pursuit. As she measured and poured, as she shopped and laundered, the woman felt tremendous pressure to do everything in a way that was perfect.

[21]But the fifties impression of what it is to be a woman, a mother, a family casts a long shadow, haunts us even if we realize it to be far from reality. Sylvia Ann Hewlett writes about interviewing President Ronald Reagan's assistant about policies toward women and children. The assistant told Hewlett that Reagan was very concerned about women and children and that his answer was to encourage the growth of the economy so that women wouldn't have to work outside the home. Hewlett points out that this idea of the fifties family dominates, despite the fact that Reagan's own mother worked in a dress shop for fourteen dollars a week to help out the family finances when young Ronald was a boy. The aberrant dream swallows the reality of his own boyhood and the reality of life today (*Lesser Life,* pp. 231-32).

[22]Quoted in ibid., p. 249.

[23]Quoted in ibid., p. 248.

[24]Betty Friedan, *The Feminine Mystique* (New York: Dell, 1963), p. 64.

[25]Coonz, *Way We Never Were,* p. 36.

[26]Dorothy L. Sayers, letter to G. G. Bell, 13.17.42, Wade Collection (Wheaton College, Wheaton, Ill.), p. 158.

[27]Friedan, *Feminine Mystique,* p. 64.

Chapter 5: Saying No to the Christian Domestic Angel

[1]Randall Ballmer, "American Fundamentalism: The Ideal of Femininity," in *Fundamentalism and Gender,* ed. John Stratton Hawley (New York: Oxford University Press, 1994), p. 59.

[2]For a helpful discussion of this issue, I suggest Rodney Clapp's *Families at the Crossroads: Beyond Traditional and Modern Options* (Downers Grove, Ill.: InterVarsity Press, 1993).

[3]Jeanette Hassey, *No Time for Silence* (Grand Rapids, Mich.: Zondervan/ Academie, 1986), p. 33. Fundamentalists were feeling increasingly out of

mainstream culture, becoming more institutionalized, taking a more literalist view of Scripture; they saw themselves as needing to stand firm against deteriorating social values.

[4]Margaret Bendroth, *Fundamentalism and Gender, 1875 to the Present* (New Haven, Conn.: Yale University Press, 1993), p. 26.

[5]Ibid.

[6]Ibid., p. 3.

[7]Ibid., pp. 3-6.

[8]Ibid., p. 75.

[9]Ibid., p. 10.

[10]Ibid., pp. 98-99.

[11]Hassey, *No Time for Silence,* p. 140.

[12]Ibid., p. 94.

[13]Ibid., p. 142.

[14]Bendroth, *Fundamentalism and Gender,* p. 76.

[15]Ibid., p. 98.

[16]Ibid., p. 78.

[17]Tammy De Villie, quoted in Ballmer, "American Fundamentalism," p. 48.

[18]Quoted in Ballmer, "American Fundamentalism," p. 4.

[19]Bendroth, *Fundamentalism and Gender,* p. 64.

[20]Ibid., p. 102.

[21]Ibid., p. 103.

[22]Ibid., p. 104.

[23]Ibid., p. 105.

[24]Quoted in ibid., p. 107.

[25]Ibid., p. 108.

[26]Ballmer, "American Fundamentalism," p. 54.

[27]Quoted in ibid.

[28]Quoted in Bendroth, *Fundamentalism and Gender,* p. 111.

[29]Quoted in Ballmer, "American Fundamentalism," p. 12.

[30]Some radio preachers are reluctantly realizing that the fifties myth can no longer be sustained. Focus on the Family has inaugurated a new magazine for single parents which takes to heart some of the challenges single parents face: living on a tight budget, trying to find time with children and so forth. And yet this realism lives side by side with nostalgia for the fifties. The April 1995 issue of *Focus on the Family* magazine includes "Holding down the Fort," a husband's article about trying to cope with the kids and household while his wife was away. The moral of this story, in which the writer admitted that women often do all these kinds of chores after a day's paid work, was that men should appreciate all the work their wives do and thank them.

There is no suggestion that they make their household a partnership.

[31]Hassey, *No Time for Silence,* p. 142.

[32]Studies show that people will experience a sense of incongruity between self and roles, especially during a time of shifts in society (Jane Attanucci, "A New Perspective on Self, Role and Relationships," in *Mapping the Moral Domain,* ed. Carol Gilligan et al. [Cambridge, Mass.: Harvard University Press, 1988], p. 202).

[33]Dorothy L. Sayers, n.d., Wade Collection, p. 486a.

Chapter 6: Becoming a Mature Disciple

[1]Quoted in Ballmer, "American Fundamentalism," p. 48.

[2]Sayers, "Not-Quite-Human Human," p. 46.

[3]See Mary Evans, *Woman in the Bible* (London: Inter-Varsity Press, 1978), and L. Swidler, *Biblical Affirmations for Women* (Philadelphia: Westminster Press, 1977).

[4]See Luke 8:1-3.

[5]See Matthew 27:55-61; Mark 15:40-47; Luke 23:49-56; John 19:25-27.

[6]In first-century Judaism, "women are sanctified through the deeds of men" (Jacob Neusner, *Method and Meaning in Ancient Judaic Studies* [Missoula, Mont.: Scholars Press, 1979], p. 101).

[7]I try to imagine what this young man might have been like if he'd followed Jesus' direction, what role he might have played in the early church.

[8]Dante, *Purgatory,* trans. and ed. Dorothy L. Sayers (London: Penguin, 1945), p. 31.

[9]Because their time has not been valued, many women have little sense of themselves as people who contribute to the common good. It becomes harder for them to ask for time to pursue meaningful tasks, and then they have less sense of themselves as productive members of society.

[10]Most women would give almost anything for uninterrupted time to pursue their calling, not to mention a space to pursue it. Houses have been arranged for years so that the only person who has no personal space within a house is the wife and mother. The husband has a den or study; the children get bedrooms and a play room or family room. Everyone hangs out in the kitchen, dining room and living room. The woman has nowhere to go and think two thoughts in a row.

When Virginia Woolf was asked to deliver a talk on what is necessary for a woman writer, she wrote a wonderfully crafted essay titled "A Room of One's Own," in which she traces the difficulties women have met in trying to become writers, historians, scholars and the like. She states that ultimately what a woman needs in order to be a writer (and by extension any other kind of creative worker) is two hundred pounds a year and a room of her own. In other words, what stops women from fulfilling their callings is often something as practical as lack of money and lack of privacy.

What women lack most often is the time alone to do what we are called to do.

History seems to bear this out. It is hard to believe that most women have simply had no gifts, say as writers, because they are genetically disposed not to write. It must not be coincidence that if we look at the women writers whom most of us have read (such as Emily and Charlotte Brontë, Jane Austen, George Eliot and Virginia Woolf), few were married, and of those, none had children.

As Sayers points out in her essay "Are Women Human?" people complain that women put family first, and yet men have never been asked to choose between job and family. We assume that the man with a wife and children will be able to do all and more than he could before his domestic bliss commenced. And this is still the case. Researchers have found that the highest-paid men have wives who do not work outside the home, who do all the domestic chores while also supplementing his social life.

The woman who marries and has children ends up making terrible decisions, trying desperately to keep her gift alive and tend the children and be there for her husband. No wonder the saying has become common: "Everyone needs a wife; no one needs a husband."

At the heart of this is the issue of whether a woman deserves to pursue her calling, whether she can claim the space and time, whether, in fact, her calling is really a calling from God and is important. She has to surmount what may seem like an incredible hurdle, and that is to say, "My time is important. My life is important. Not just as it is used to please and serve others. My calling is important. Even though I am not a man." A woman may not realize how revolutionary this idea is until she tries to implement it in her life. She will find herself apologizing to everyone—to the one she has hired to help her with housework, to the child-care helper, to her children, to the school, to her church and perhaps most of all to her husband. ("I'm sorry that it's leftovers again tonight." "I'm sorry the laundry is not done." "I'm sorry we're out of cookies.")

Chapter 7: Unmasking Our Identity

[1]Erik Erikson, *Identity, Youth and Crisis* (New York: W. W. Norton, 1968), p. 278.

[2]Rachel T. Hare-Mustin and Jeanne Marecek, *Making a Difference: Psychology and the Construction of Gender* (New Haven, Conn.: Yale University

Press, 1990), p. 10.

3Susan Brownmiller, *Femininity* (New York: Fawcett Columbine, 1984), pp. 34-35.

4Sherry Bunge Mortenson, unpublished study, Bethel College, 1994.

5Harriet Goldhor Lerner, *The Dance of Deception* (New York: HarperCollins, 1994), pp. 181-82.

6Ibid., p. 185.

7Adrienne Rich, *On Lies, Secrets and Silence* (New York: W. W. Norton, 1975), p. 188.

8Doug Frank, "The Strangely Distant God of American Evangelicals," lectures presented at the McKenzie Study Center, Eugene, Oregon, October 2-3, 1992.

9Julius H. Rubin, in his book *Religious Melancholy and Protestant Experience in America* (New York: Oxford University Press, 1994), points out that much religious teaching, for instance of the Puritans, pressured adherents to endless soul-searching, to endless searching for their own sins and shortcomings. To the true believer, self-loathing was a goal: "The very humility of the saint hath a high design: when they be in the dust, in self-abhorrence and self-condemnation, they are aspiring thence as high as heaven: their humble confession, and tears, and groans, have a tendency to that glory, which is above the sun" (Richard Baxter, *Treatise of Conversion,* quoted in ibid.).

Just like Baxter, the audiences I question about how they feel about God's love imply that they know God loves them but that endless self-flagellation, dislike, loathing is the way to glory. These responses show a sense of fundamental lack of self-respect. They indicate what many contemporary psychologists would call shame-based thinking; that is, our sense of what is lacking in ourselves has little to do with our actions and much to do with a sense of our inner selves as loathsome.

10Frank, "Strangely Distant God," p. 2.

Chapter 8: Stepping out of Roles and off the Pedestal

1Lisa Sinclair, "The Role of Unresolved Anger in the Psychosocial Functioning of Missionary Wives," master's thesis, Columbia Biblical Seminary, November 1991.

2Jean Baker Miller, *Toward a New Psychology of Women* (Boston: Beacon, 1976), pp. 29-35.

3Ibid., p. 122.

4Mason, *Making Our Lives Our Own,* p. 8.

5Ruthellen Josselson, *Finding Herself: Pathways to Identity Development in Women* (San Francisco: Jossey Bass, 1987), p. 179.

6David Adams, *Cry of the Deer* (London: Triangle/SPCK, 1987), pp. 38-39.

Chapter 9: Finding Our God-Given Calling

[1]Stephen Covey, *The Seven Habits of Highly Effective People: Restoring the Character Ethic* (New York: Simon & Schuster, 1989), p. 128.

[2]See Swidler, *Biblical Affirmations,* and Evans, *Woman in the Bible.*

[3]Dorothy L. Sayers, "Vocation in Work," in Wade Collection, p. 89. Abridged from address delivered at the Dome, Brighton, March 8, 1941.

[4]Viktor Frankl, quoted in Mihaly Csikszentmihalyi, *Flow: The Psychology of Optimal Experience* (New York: Harper Perennial, 1990), p. 2.

[5]Csikszentmihalyi, *Flow,* pp. 3-4.

[6]Ibid., pp. 158-59.

[7]When girls this age are given multiple-choice tests they score higher than boys—unless the option "Not sure" is added to their choices. Girls choose this option so frequently that their scores sink far below boys' scores (for more information on this topic, see Carol Gilligan, *Meeting at the Crossroads* [Cambridge, Mass.: Harvard University Press, 1992], or Mary Pipher, *Reviving Ophelia: Saving the Selves of Adolescent Girls* [New York: Putnam, 1994]). Some psychologists believe that girls become so concerned with peer acceptance that they lose a sense of what they believe. For instance, Barbara Kerr, an expert on gifted girls, says that usually gifted girls are encouraged by parents and teachers to lower their sights (*Smart Girls, Gifted Women* [Columbus, Ohio: Psychology, 1985], p. 23). Even the most gifted have vague career goals. Being a female is something that gifted girls can adjust to, according to Kerr, just like any other disability (*Smart Girls, Gifted Women,* p. 141).

Many women suffer from lack of self-confidence, in general underestimating their abilities, while males overestimate theirs. Women tend to become fearful and anxious when things go well, expecting that something must go wrong. When women succeed they feel they should apologize for it, or they assume that their success is not really a big thing, that everyone knew what they discovered anyhow. Women constantly express doubts about their competence and abilities (Irene P. Stiver, "Work Inhibitions in Women," in *Women's Growth in Connection,* ed. Judith V. Jordan et al. [New York: Guilford, 1991], p. 225). Studies show that women tend to overlook new challenges in working situations; they rarely seek advancement, usually doing for others before themselves (Stiver, "Work Inhibitions," pp. 227-28).

Bright boys see their futures in very positive terms; bright girls do not (Stiver, "Work Inhibitions," p. 223). Studies show that although parents wanted their daughters to be educated, they didn't encourage them to pursue careers as they did their sons (Josselson, *Finding Herself,* p. 36). Most of the girls in college who were studied "could not imagine their lives years later, even with respect to a geographical locale"; their flexibility and inter-personal skills were high, but "how they would express this identity awaited the circumstances that would unfold" (Josselson, *Finding Herself,* p. 39).

[8]Because I am an introvert, I cannot judge my gifts or calling by how I feel before I do something. Any time I'm going to give a talk, lead a retreat or teach, I feel a sense of dread. I would much prefer to stay home and read and think and write and ponder the mysteries. My reservations, my dread, have to do with mustering the energy to go into a situation where there are lots of people. My energy level during and after a talk or retreat is more of an indication of my gifts and calling.

[9]Sayers, "Vocation in Work."

[10]Parker Palmer, *The Active Life* (San Francisco: Harper, 1990), p. 20.

[11]Mary Rose O'Reilly, *The Peaceable Classroom* (Portsmouth, N.H.: Boyn-ton/Cook [Heinemann], 1993), pp. 89-92.

Chapter 10: Relationships & Calling

[1]In Carol Gilligan's landmark studies of men and women's moral decision-making (*In a Different Voice* [Cambridge, Mass.: Harvard University Press, 1982]), she showed that men tend to perceive greater threat in situations of connection and relationships; women, on the other hand, perceive more threat in situations of achievement and independence. Subsequent studies have confirmed this.

[2]Psychologists Grace Baruch, Rosalind Barnett and Caryl Rivers studied thousands of women to find three areas that point to a woman's having a sense of well-being: self-esteem, a sense of control over one's life and the absence of anxiety or depression. These researchers broke their subjects down into a number of categories based on marital status, parental status and work status. What they discovered was how important balance is for women.

The most vulnerable woman, according to this study, is the married wom-an with children at home. She is almost entirely dependent for her self-esteem on her husband's approval. She is more prone to anxiety and depres-sion than any of the other women studied, and usually the least qualified for work. If she were to lose her husband by divorce or death (which is statis-tically very likely), she would be unable to cope.

The highest level of satisfaction was among those who were married with children and employed outside the home. With two spheres into which to pour their energies, such women are able to lead lives balanced between calling and relationships.

In their extensive studies of women they found that while some women thought they could achieve a greater sense of well-being through changing life circumstances, what they really needed was a sense of mastery. This sense of mastery was often based on developing a sense of agency, the sense that they could begin to make some choices. See Grace K. Baruch, Rosalind Barnett and Caryl Rivers, *Lifeprints: New Patterns of Love & Work for Today's Woman* (New York: McGraw-Hill, 1983), p. 17.

3Janet L. Surrey, "The 'Self-in-Relation': A Theory of Women's Development," in *Women's Growth in Connection,* ed. Judith V. Jordan et al. (New York: Guilford, 1991), p. 52.

4Although this has often been seen as a variation on women's intuition, it is actually "highly complex affective and cognitive functioning" (Judith V. Jordan, Janet L. Surrey and Alexandra Kaplan, "Women and Empathy: Implications for Psychological Development and Psychotherapy," in *Women's Growth in Connection,* ed. Judith V. Jordan et al., pp. 28-30).

5Many women psychologists believe that the emphasis on individuality that has characterized thinking about moral decision-making is inadequate and focuses too much on a male detachment that women do not attain or aspire to (Gilligan, *In a Different Voice,* p. 6).

6Ibid., p. 4.

7Miller, *Toward a New Psychology,* p. 184.

8Alexandra G. Kaplan, "The 'Self-in-Relation': Implications for Depression in Women," in *Women's Growth in Connection,* ed. Judith V. Jordan et al. (New York: Guilford, 1991), p. 202.

9Miller, *Toward a New Psychology,* pp. 50-52.

10Ibid., p. 40.

11Marilyn Peterson, *At Personal Risk: Boundary Violations in Professional/ Client Relationships* (New York: W. W. Norton, 1992), p. 12.

12Mason, *Making Our Lives Our Own,* p. 81.

13Jean Vanier, *Community and Growth* (New York: Paulist, 1989), chap. 1.

14Henri Nouwen, *The Road to Daybreak* (Garden City, N.Y.: Doubleday, 1990), p. 184.

Chapter 11: Motherhood & Personhood

1A woman wants to hear Jesus praise the institution of motherhood, and she calls out a well-known chant: "Blessed is the womb that bore you and the breasts that nursed you!" Jesus retorts immediately: "Blessed rather are those who hear the word of God and obey it" (Luke 11:27-28). When someone in a crowd tells Jesus that his mother and siblings are outside, Jesus says, "My mother and my brothers are those who hear the word of God and do it" (Luke 8:19-21). He talks of hating family compared to the kingdom of

God and of a sword that will divide families.

[2]Sara Ruddick, *Maternal Thinking* (Boston: Beacon, 1989), p. 17.

[3]Ibid., p. 20.

[4]Lerner, *Dance of Deception*, p. 94.

[5]It is arguable that the woman who sits in her leisured home ministering to a child's every whim can do that only because somewhere a woman is working harder and children are having shorter childhoods. "The middle-class Victorian family depended for its existence on the multiplication of those families who were too poor and powerless to retreat into their own little oases and who therefore had to provision the oases of others. Childhood was prolonged for the nineteenth century middle class only because it was drastically foreshortened for the other sections of the population" (Coontz, *Way We Never Were*, p. 11).

The spread of textile mills and the working of the poor and children in these mills "freed" middle-class women from the hardest of their household tasks—making cloth; but only at the expense of workers in the factories, half of whom were children under eleven in 1845 (ibid.). Perhaps we can buy our children the Nikes they want only because a ten-year-old is making twenty cents an hour in Korea making them.

[6]Mason, *Making Our Lives*, p. 83.

[7]Baruch, Barnett and Rivers, *Lifeprints*, pp. 43-44.

[8]Miller, *Toward a New Psychology*, p. 65.

[9]Ibid., p. 73.

[10]Ibid., p. 66.

[11]Ibid., p. 71.

[12]Nancy Chodorow, *The Reproduction of Mothering* (Berkeley: University of California Press, 1978).

[13]Annie Dillard, *An American Childhood* (New York: Harper Perennial, 1988), pp. 148-49.

[14]Covey, *Seven Habits of Highly Effective People*, pp. 112-13.

Chapter 12: Meaningful Work & Real Rest

[1]Joan Chittister, *Wisdom Distilled from the Daily: Living the Rule of St. Benedict Today* (San Francisco: Harper, 1991), p. 83.

[2]Some thinkers see the Reformation as disastrous to the human understanding of work. "The Puritan assumption that all action disagreeable to the doer is ipso facto more meritorious than enjoyable action is firmly rooted in the exaggerated valuation set on pride. I do not mean that there is no nobility in doing unpleasant things from a sense of duty, but only that there is more nobility in doing them gladly out a sheer love of the job" (Dorothy L. Sayers,

The Mind of the Maker [Westport, Conn.: Greenwood, 1970], p. 92).

[3]Edith Fassell, *Working Ourselves to Death* (New York: Harper Paperbacks, 1990), p. 2.

[4]Juliet Schor, *The Overworked American* (New York: BasicBooks, 1991), p. 122.

[5]Matthew Fox, *The Reinvention of Work* (San Francisco: Harper, 1994).

[6]Quoted in Witold Rybczynski, *Waiting for the Weekend* (New York: Viking, 1991), p. 51.

[7]Chittister, *Wisdom Distilled from the Daily*, p. 84.

[8]The opposite of such joy was the medieval idea of the deadly sin of acedia, which really meant depression, listlessness, triviality.

[9]Chittister, *Wisdom Distilled from the Daily*, p. 85.

[10]Ibid., pp. 91-93.

[11]Dorothy L. Sayers, *Why Work?* (London: Methuen, 1942), p. 16.

[12]The shattering of the ideal of work and calling as synonymous came with capitalism, argues Ellul, because now work is bought and sold; work is separated from workmanship. Sayers argues that if the image of God on humanity is the urge and need to create, the Fall is the fact that people have to work to eat. The linking of work and money is what taints the relationship.

[13]Dorothee Soelle and Shirley A. Cloyes, *To Work and Love: A Theology of Creation* (Philadelphia: Fortress, 1984).

[14]Chittister, *Wisdom Distilled from the Daily*, p. 102.

Chapter 13: Through All the Changing Scenes of Life

[1]Josselson, *Finding Herself,* pp. 64-65.

[2]" 'What,' men have asked distractedly from the beginning of time, 'what on earth do women want?' I do not know that women, *as* women, want anything in particular, but as human beings they want, my good men, exactly what you want yourselves: interesting occupation, reasonable freedom for their pleasures, and a sufficient emotional outlet. What form the occupation, the pleasures and the emotion may take, depends entirely upon the individual. You know that this is so with yourselves—why will you not believe that it is so with us?" says Sayers in her essay "Are Women Human?" (p. 32).

[3]Peg Thompson, *Finding Your Own Spiritual Path* (Minneapolis: Hazelden, 1994), p. 186.